Columbia University

Contributions to Education

Teachers College Series

No. 459

AMS PRESS
NEW YORK

A BASIS FOR BUILDING A COURSE IN ECONOMICS OF THE HOME

DERIVING DESIRABLE CONTENT BY THE USE OF LOCAL FAMILY CASE STUDIES

By

FRANCES HOWE LEIGHTON, Ph.D.

Teachers College, Columbia University
Contributions to Education, No. 459

Bureau of Publications
Teachers College, Columbia University
NEW YORK CITY
1931

Library of Congress Cataloging in Publication Data

Leighton, Frances Howe, 1898-
A basis for building a course in economics of the home.

Reprint of the 1931 ed., issued in series: Teachers College, Columbia University. Contributions to education, no. 459.
Originally presented as the author's thesis, Columbia.
Includes bibliographical references.
1. Cost and standard of living--United States.
2. Consumption (Economics)--United States. 3. Home economics--Study and teaching. I. Title. II. Series: Columbia University. Teachers College. Contributions to education, no. 459.

HD6983.L44 1972 301.15'43'6407 74-176983
ISBN 0-404-55459-8

Reprinted by Special Arrangement with Teachers College Press, New York, New York

From the edition of 1931, New York
First AMS edition published in 1972
Manufactured in the United States

AMS PRESS, INC.
NEW YORK, N. Y. 10003

ACKNOWLEDGMENT

The writer wishes to acknowledge her indebtedness and express her gratitude to all who have coöperated in and assisted with the preparation of this study. She is especially indebted to the many families who have given so generously of their time. She welcomes this opportunity to express her appreciation to Professor Frederick G. Bonser, the chairman of her dissertation committee, for his unfailing interest, patience, and encouragement at every point in the study, and to Professors Cora M. Winchell, Benjamin Andrews, and Harold F. Clark for their helpful criticisms.

F. H. L.

CONTENTS

PART I

PART II

PART III

TABLES

PART I

CHAPTER I

STATEMENT OF THE PROBLEM

This is a study to ascertain, in the light of our changing economic life, what material should be included in a course in the economics of consumption using the problems of everyday family life as the central theme. An attempt has been made through personal interviews with selected families to determine the problems the solution of which would aid in a more efficient use of their income, better household management, and thereby a higher standard of living. A large portion of the waste of our economic order rises, after goods have been produced, from poorly arranged consumption, which results not only in the loss of satisfaction and enjoyment on the part of those who consume poorly, but in a misuse of productive resources as well.

Consumption is a complicated process which covers a wide range of activities. It deals with problems in human behavior and in human motives which might seem to belong more properly in the field of the psychologist than in that of the economist. "Consumption has been defined as the science which deals with the administration of resources in the satisfaction of human wants, in so far as this administration involves consideration of price or cost."[1]

The economics of consumption, from a social point of view, is concerned with three major problems. The first of these is an analysis of the status of the consumer in the existing economic order. For example, the goods which are produced depend upon the desires of certain consumers. At the same time the economic order limits and conditions consumption in many ways. The quantities of goods which a person may command are limited by his income. His choices are materially influenced by advertising and salesmanship. The range of choices depends, in a large measure, upon what others

[1] Waite, Warren C. *Economics of Consumption*, p. 4. McGraw-Hill Book Company, Inc., New York. 1928.

consume. His choices and activities are modified on every side by the economic order in which he finds himself. Second, in a study of the economics of consumption there is the problem of the manner in which goods are chosen by the consumer and the effects of these choices upon the economic order. While the explanation of choice must rest, in a major part, upon psychology, the economist deals primarily with the modification of these choices by prices, and the effect of changes in choices upon prices. Third, there is the problem of the relation of human welfare to wealth. This is frequently a matter of consumption in its desirable and undesirable modes. There are also certain problems of social control and social betterment which are primarily problems of consumption. The principal economic problem in consumption, from the individual point of view, is the proper administration of the individual income.

This study is restricted to the second and third problems in an attempt to show the patterns into which expenditures fall under given conditions in families of limited means and the changes which they would like to make in order to gain greater satisfaction from the use of their incomes. It presents their own problems, many of which deal directly with the proper administration of their incomes and others which relate to the manner of choosing goods and to problems of social control and social betterment.

The problem of the individual as a consumer is becoming more complex, for the kinds and qualities of goods offered in the market are constantly increasing. As a producer, on the contrary, his task is becoming simpler; for instead of producing a range of products, he is usually a specialist in the production of a small part of a single article. The great development in technique which has taken place in production during the last century and a half has no parallel in consumption. There are two principal reasons for this fact: first, the very nature of the consumption problems precludes the use of exact measures for testing the results of individual expenditures; second, the home, which is the usual unit considered in consumption, is too small to function well economically.

A large part of all the study that has been made in the field of consumption has been done in terms of standards of living. These are as numerous as the people in the world, yet within certain groups they tend to array themselves about an average. For this reason we speak of the standards of living of different social groups—the standard, for example, of the professional classes, or of farmers.

Or we speak of the standard of living of different races, geographic regions, or nationalities. While grouping on the basis of money income is the most arbitrary, it is the most convenient method of studying standards of living.

One may define a standard of living as the sum total, not of things, but of satisfactions. A standard of living has seven essential elements: (1) safety, (2) health, (3) shelter, (4) employment, (5) education, (6) recreation, (7) spiritual and aesthetic expression. The plane of living depends roughly on the attainment of these essential elements.[2] The cost of living depends on how people live, as well as on the prices of what they consume. The manner of the consumption of goods may be even more distinctive and characteristic of the differences in the standards of living than the actual goods consumed. In 1926 the National Industrial Conference Board made a study of the cost of living in New York City. The study shows how much it costs to maintain families of varying sizes in that city, but it does not consider the standard of living on any other basis than that of money income and expenditure. This present study is undertaken to show a picture of the standards of living of a selected group of families from the problems which they raise in their effort to meet the seven elements listed above, which are considered essential if one accepts the definition of a standard of living as the sum total, not of things, but of satisfactions.

Summary

This is a study to ascertain, through personal interviews with a selected group of families, problems the solution of which would make for a higher standard of living. A standard of living is defined as the sum total, not of things, but of satisfactions, and as such is made up of seven elements: safety, health, shelter, employment, education, recreation, and spiritual and aesthetic expression.

[2] Eliot, Thomas T. "Present-Day Social Problems of the American Family." *Journal of Home Economics*, Vol. 20, No. 4, pp. 229-237, April, 1928.

CHAPTER II

BASIS OF SELECTION OF THE 75 FAMILIES, AND METHOD USED IN THIS STUDY

Before selecting families for study an attempt was made to eliminate as many as possible of the causes of variations among them. A review of the studies which have been made on standards of living shows that the following are the chief reasons for the differences in results and make for difficulty in comparing studies.

1. *Personal or individual differences.* Since it is impossible to eliminate personal and individual differences in familes, it had to be assumed that if as many as possible of the other differences were eliminated, these differences would not be so noticeable.

2. *Geographic differences.* There is a wide variation between the standards of living of people in different parts of the same country. For that reason the families were chosen from New York City so as to have them all within a close area.

3. *Occupational and social differences.* Standards of living vary considerably with occupations. Generally such differences may be accounted for by differences in earnings. For that reason families were chosen whose income levels were similar.

4. *Differences due to education and natural ability.* There are undoubtedly considerable differences in the standards of living due to differences in education, skill, and managing ability of the heads of families. There is very little information available to show just how much difference education and skill in household management make in the standard of living. Kirkpatrick, in *Farmers' Standard of Living,* has worked out the distribution of expenditures for the main items, clothing, food, rent, etc., in accordance with the amount of education of the farm operators and homemakers.[1] In the *Cost of Living Studies* of the California State Civil Service Commission, published in 1923, it was assumed that 5 per cent might be deducted from the usual amount necessary to support a family if household

[1] Kirkpatrick, E. L. *Farmer's Standard of Living.* U. S. Department of Agriculture, Bulletin No. 1466, pp. 44, 45.

management were carefully and skillfully undertaken.[2] Nystrom estimates that 10 per cent might be saved by a well-educated and experienced housekeeper, and the same standard of living maintained.[3]

5. *Variations due to difference in size of family and income.* Various budget studies which have been made in the past show that the small family makes less demand upon the family income for the necessaries of life, for care and education, and for the cost of illness. The difference in the size of the family must make differences in the distribution of the family income and in the plane of living of the family. For that reason the size of the family was a factor in the selection of the families for this study.

For the foregoing reasons the following bases of selection were accepted for this investigation:

Number of families: Twenty-five families on each of the following income levels: $900-$1,600; $1,600-$2,300; $2,300-$3,000.

Size of family: Father, mother, and from 2 to 4 children, no one of whom is over 14 years of age.

Length of time in this country: The homemakers must have been born in this country.

Occupational types: A reasonable proportion of wage-earners in the professional, commercial, and industrial occupations.

Education: At least one, the father or the mother, must have attended college or graduated from high school.

Geographical distribution: All the families were chosen from the Borough of Manhattan, New York City.

Method Used in this Study

The interview method was used throughout the investigation. The same interviewer met all the families. In 85 per cent of the cases she interviewed the husband and wife together. In the 15 per cent of the cases where the husband or the wife was not present during the interview, the interviewer gave a list of the problems emerging from the first interview to the one who had not been present

[2] Heller Committee for Research in Social Economics. *Cost of Living Studies,* p. 1. University of California Press, 1928.

[3] Nystrom, P. H. *Economic Principles of Consumption,* p. 261. Ronald Press, New York, 1929.

when a second or third visit was made to the house. In no case was a list of problems emerging from an interview with one family given to any other family. The methods common to all interviews listed in Richmond's *Social Diagnosis*[4] were used in this study. They are as follows:

1. Strive to procure from each the evidence that each is best able to give.
2. Utilize any natural avenue of approach to a client presented at the beginning of the interview, and as the interview develops avoid the temptation to shape it in accordance with preconceived ideas of its probable content. The same caution applies to any questions we may have to ask—the way in which we put our question should not suggest the answer.
3. Give the person interviewed ample time, therefore, in which to explain his own point of view, and give him also a sympathetic hearing.
4. Our ability to show genuine interest will play an important part in procuring both information and backing.

Table 1 shows the occupational distribution of the principal wage-earners in the 75 families. There are 25 families in each of the three income levels, with the number of families representing the professional, commercial, and industrial groups within these income levels as nearly equal as possible.

In order to make for a more homogeneous grouping of families, it was decided that at least one of the parents, either the father or the mother, must have attended college or graduated from high school. Table 2 shows the last year of school attended by the men and women.

Table 3 shows the distribution of income according to size of families.

Since budget studies which have been made in the past show variations in the distribution of the family income due to differences in the size of the family, it was decided that the families interviewed for this study should be limited to those families with two, three, and four children. These children should be under fourteen years of age, which tends to bring all the families into a closer age group. There are 43 families with 2 children, 25 with 3, and 7 families with 4 children.

The parents and children in the 75 families interviewed were all born in this country with the exception of one woman who was brought to this country as a baby. Among the 150 men and women interviewed, the Scotch, Scotch-Irish and Irish comprised 70, which

[4] Richmond, Mary E. *Social Diagnosis,* p. 342. Russell Sage Foundation, New York, 1917.

TABLE 1

OCCUPATIONAL DISTRIBUTION OF PRINCIPAL WAGE-EARNER IN THE 75 FAMILIES

Distribution of Occupations	*Number in Each Occupation*	*Income Level*		
		$900 to $1,600	*$1,600 to $2,300*	*$2,300 to $3,000*
PROFESSIONAL				
1. Musician	9	3	4	2
2. Accountant	1	--	--	1
3. Tutor	1	--	--	1
4. Free-lance writer	3	--	1	2
5. Private school teacher	1	--	--	1
6. Hebrew teacher	1	1	--	--
7. Private secretary	2	--	1	1
8. Bookkeeper and secretary	2	1	1	--
Total	20	5	7	8
COMMERCIAL (SKILLED)				
9. Cashier	6	4	1	1
10. Clerk	1	--	--	1
11. Tailor shop worker	2	1	1	--
12. Carpenter	1	--	--	1
13. Postal clerk	1	--	1	--
14. Patrolman	7	--	4	3
15. Electrician	4	2	1	1
16. Mason	1	--	--	1
17. Radio mechanic	2	--	--	2
Total	25	7	8	10
INDUSTRIAL (UNSKILLED)				
18. Garment factory worker	12	4	2	6
19. Bill collector	1	--	1	--
20. News-stand dealer	2	1	1	--
21. Carpet sewer	1	1	--	--
22. Bricklayer's helper	1	--	--	1
23. Pastry cook's helper	2	1	1	--
24. Cafeteria counter man	1	--	1	--
25. Slaughterhouse worker	1	1	--	--
26. Street cleaner	1	1	--	--
27. Truck driver	3	2	1	--
28. Scene shifter	1	--	1	--
29. Taxicab driver	1	1	--	--
30. Teamster	1	1	--	--
31. Window cleaner	1	--	1	--
32. Garbage collector	1	--	1	--
Total	30	13	10	7
TOTAL	75	25	25	25

TABLE 2

LAST YEAR OF SCHOOL ATTENDED BY THE 75 MEN AND 75 WOMEN OF VARIOUS INCOME LEVELS

Last Year of School Attended	*Income Level*						*Total Number of Men and Women*
	$900 to $1,600		*$1,600 to $2,300*		*$2,300 to $3,000*		
	Men	*Women*	*Men*	*Women*	*Men*	*Women*	
Grade							
6th grade	2	1	4	2	--	--	9
7th grade	2	1	2	--	2	--	7
8th grade	1	1	1	1	--	--	4
Parochial or private school	1	1	--	1	--	--	3
High school							
1st year	3	1	1	--	1	1	7
2nd year	2	1	1	1	2	1	8
3rd year	4	4	4	4	3	3	22
4th year	8	9	10	13	14	11	65
College	--	2	2	1	3	2	10
Not designated	2	4	--	2	--	7	15
TOTAL	25	25	25	25	25	25	150

number, with the 2 Welsh and 20 English, makes up 61 per cent of the entire group. When the interviewer was trying to find families to meet the criteria previously outlined, no attempt was made to limit the study to any one nationality. The distribution by nationality is shown in Table 4.

Table 5 summarizes for the 75 families the occupation of the wage-earner, the income range, number of children in the family, the last year of school attended by man and wife, and, in addition, the time spent by the wife in home economics courses.

SUMMARY

The 75 families selected for this study meet the following criteria:

1. *Length of time in this country.* At least the second generation, so that standards of living due to racial differences and background are somewhat eliminated by the time spent in this country.

2. *Occupational types.* As nearly as possible an equal number of

TABLE 3

DISTRIBUTION OF INCOME ACCORDING TO SIZE OF FAMILIES

Distribution of Income	*Number of Members in Family*			*Total Number of Families in Each Income Level*
	Man, Wife, and Two Children	*Man, Wife, and Three Children*	*Man, Wife, and Four Children*	
	4	*5*	*6*	
$900–$1,600				
$ 900–$1,100	2	1	--	3
$1,100–$1,300	3	3	--	6
$1,300–$1,500	6	3	--	9
$1,500–$1,600	3	2	2	7
Total	14	9	2	25
$1,600–$2,300				
$1,600–$1,700	3	3	--	6
$1,700–$1,900	2	2	1	5
$1,900–$2,100	4	2	--	6
$2,100–$2,300	5	2	1	8
Total	14	9	2	25
$2,300–$3,000				
$2,300–$2,500	2	1	--	3
$2,500–$2,700	3	3	2	8
$2,700–$2,900	4	1	--	5
$2,900–$3,000	6	2	1	9
Total	15	7	3	25
TOTAL	43	25	7	75

wage-earners in the professional, commercial, and industrial occupations.

3. *Education.* At least one of the parents had attended college or graduated from high school.

4. *Location.* All of the families were living in New York City and all had been living in the city from four to ten years.

5. *Family group.* All of the families are complete groups in that each consists of both parents and from two to four children. None of the children are over fourteen years of age, a fact which eliminates the problem of child labor.

6. *Income.* The 75 families interviewed are equally distributed

TABLE 4

RACIAL BACKGROUND OF THE MEN AND WOMEN IN THE 75 FAMILIES INTERVIEWED

	Income Level						Total Number of Men and Women
	$900 to $1,600		*$1,600 to $2,300*		*$2,300 to $3,000*		
	Men	*Women*	*Men*	*Women*	*Men*	*Women*	
Welsh	--	--	--	--	1	1	2
Scotch	2	--	3	Eng. Des.	5	3	
Scotch-Irish	3	6	4	16	3	2	70
Irish	7	--	6	--	8	2	
German	3	--	2	3	3	2	13
Hebrew	1	1	--	--	--	--	2
English	4	--	6	--	2	8	20
Italian	5	5	2	2	1	1	16
Not designated	--	13	2	4	2	6	27
TOTAL	25	25	25	25	25	25	150

in each of the following income levels: $900-$1,600; $1,600-$2,300; $2,300-$3,000.

The 75 families were interviewed by the author. In 85 per cent of the interviews the husband and the wife were both present and contributed problems. In the 15 per cent of the cases where the husband or the wife was not present during the interview, the interviewer gave a list of the problems emerging from the first interview to the one who had been absent when an appointment was made for a second interview. All the families knew that the object of the interview was to obtain from them problems relating to their standard of living. The interviewer explained in each case what was meant by the definition of a standard of living, and definitely led the conversation in each interview to the seven essential elements of a standard of living outlined in Chapter I.

TABLE 5

OCCUPATION, INCOME, NUMBER OF CHILDREN, AND EDUCATION OF EACH OF THE 75 FAMILIES INTERVIEWED

Occupation	*Income Range*	*Number of Children*	*Last Year of School Attended by*		*Length of Time Spent by the Wife in Home Economics Courses*
			Man	*Wife*	
Musician	$ 900–$1,100	2	H. S. 3 Yr.	College 1 Yr.	1 Year
Musician	900– 1,100	2	H. S. 1 Yr.	H. S. Grad.	1 Year
News-stand dealer	900– 1,100	3	Not Desig.	H. S. Grad.	1 Year
Garment factory worker	1,100– 1,300	3	H. S. Grad.	H. S. Grad.	½ Year
Truck driver	1,100– 1,300	2	Paroch. Sch.	H. S. Grad.	--
Garment factory worker	1,100– 1,300	3	H. S. 3 Yr.	H. S. Grad.	1 Year
Garment factory worker	1,100– 1,300	2	6th Grade	H. S. Grad.	--
Cashier	1,100– 1,300	3	H. S. 1 Yr.	H. S. Grad.	1 Year
Slaughterhouse worker	1,100– 1,300 part-time	2	7th Grade	H. S. Grad.	1 Year
Musician	1,300– 1,500	2	H. S. Grad.	College 1 Yr.	2 Years
Tailor shop worker	1,300– 1,500	2	8th Grade	H. S. Grad.	½ Year
Pastry cook	1,300– 1,500	3	H. S. Grad.	H. S. Grad.	½ Year
Garment factory worker	1,300– 1,500	3	7th Grade	H. S. Grad.	--
Taxicab driver	1,300– 1,500	2	Not Desig.	H. S. Grad.	--
Cashier	1,300– 1,500	2	H. S. 2 Yr.	H. S. Grad.	1 Year
Cashier	1,300– 1,500	2	H. S. 2 Yr.	H. S. Grad.	1 Year
Street cleaner	1,300– 1,500	2	6th Grade	H. S. Grad.	--
Truck driver	1,300– 1,500	3	H. S. 3 Yr.	H. S. Grad.	1 Year
Hebrew teacher	1,500– 1,600	4	H. S. Grad.	6th Grade	--
Bookkeeper and secretary	1,500– 1,600	2	H. S. Grad.	Private Sch.	2 Years
Cashier	1,500– 1,600	3	H. S. Grad.	8th Grade	--
Teamster	1,500– 1,600	4	H. S. 1 Yr.	H. S. Grad.	--
Carpet sewer	1,500– 1,600	3	H. S. Grad.	7th Grade	--
Electrician	1,500– 1,600	2	H. S. Grad.	H. S. Grad.	--
Electrician	1,500 part-time	2	H. S. 3 Yr.	H. S. Grad.	--
Cafeteria counter man	1,600– 1,700	3	H. S. 1 Yr.	H. S. Grad.	--
Musician	1,600– 1,700	3	H. S. Grad.	6th Grade	--
Tailor shop worker	1,600– 1,700	2	H. S. 3 Yr.	H. S. Grad.	1 Year
Garment factory worker	1,600– 1,700	2	6th Grade	H. S. Grad.	1 Year
Garment factory worker	1,600– 1,700	2	7th Grade	H. S. Grad.	--
News-stand dealer	1,600– 1,700	3	H. S. 3 Yr.	H. S. Grad.	1 Year
Musician	1,700– 1,900	2	H. S. 2 Yr.	H. S. Grad.	--
Musician	1,700– 1,900	2	8th Grade	H. S. Grad.	1 Year
Patrolman (1st 3 Yr.)	1,700– 1,900	3	H. S. Grad.	Not Desig.	--
Bill collector	1,700– 1,900	3	7th Grade	H. S. Grad.	1 Year
Scene shifter	1,700– 1,900	4	7th Grade	H. S. Grad.	½ Year
Free-lance writer	1,900– 2,100	2	College 1 Yr.	Not Desig.	--
Cashier	1,900– 2,100	2	H. S. Grad.	H. S. 3 Yr.	½ Year
Postal clerk	1,900– 2,100	2	H. S. Grad.	8th Grade	--
Garbage collector	1,900– 2,100	2	Not Desig.	H. S. Grad.	--
Patrolman (4th Yr.)	1,900– 2,100	3	H. S. Grad.	6th Grade	--
Patrolman (4th Yr.)	1,900– 2,100	3	H. S. Grad.	H. S. 2 Yr.	--
Patrolman (2nd Half-5 Yr.)	2,100– 2,300	2	H. S. Grad.	Private Sch.	2 Years
Electrician	2,100– 2,300	2	H. S. Grad.	H. S. 3 Yr.	--

TABLE 5 (*Continued*)

Occupation	*Income Range*	*Number of Children*	*Last Year of School Attended by*		*Length of Time Spent by the Wife in Home Economics Courses*
			Man	*Wife*	
Pastry cook	$2,100–$2,300	3	6th Grade	H. S. Grad.	--
Truck driver	2,100– 2,300	2	H. S. 3 Yr.	H. S. Grad.	--
Musician	2,100– 2,300	4	H. S. 3 Yr.	College 1 Yr.	2 Years
Private secretary	2,100– 2,300	2	College 1 Yr.	H. S. 3 Yr.	--
Window cleaner	2,100– 2,300	2	6th Grade	H. S. Grad.	1 Year
Bookkeeper and secretary	2,100– 2,300	3	H. S. Grad.	H. S. 3 Yr.	--
Garment factory worker	2,300– 2,500	2	7th Grade	H. S. Grad.	1 Year
Garment factory worker	2,300– 2,500	2	H. S. 1 Yr.	H. S. Grad.	--
Garment factory worker	2,300– 2,500	3	H. S. 3 Yr.	H. S. Grad.	1 Year
Garment foreman	2,500– 2,700	2	H. S. 2 Yr.	H. S. Grad.	1 Year
Musician	2,500– 2,700	2	H. S. Grad.	Not Definite	--
Patrolman	2,500– 2,700	2	H. S. Grad.	Not Definite	--
Bricklayer	2,500– 2,700	3	H. S. 2 Yr.	H. S. Grad.	--
Garment factory worker (Notions)	2,500– 2,700	3	H. S. Grad.	Not Definite	--
Patrolman	2,500– 2,700	3	H. S. Grad.	Not Definite	--
Garment factory worker	2,500– 2,700	4	7th Grade	H. S. Grad.	--
Patrolman	2,500– 2,700	4	H. S. Grad.	Not Definite	--
Musician	2,700– 2,900	2	H. S. Grad.	H. S. Grad.	½ Year
Private secretary	2,700– 2,900	2	H. S. Grad.	H. S. 3 Yr.	--
Free-lance writer	2,700– 2,900	2	H. S. Grad.	H. S. 3 Yr.	--
Tutor	2,700– 2,900	2	College	H. S. Grad.	½ Year special homemakers' course
Radio mechanic	2,700– 2,900	3	H. S. Grad.	H. S. 2 Yr.	--
Clerk (type not desig.)	2,900– 3,000	2	H. S. Grad.	Not Desig.	½ Year
Carpenter	2,900– 3,000	2	H. S. 3 Yr.	H. S. Grad.	--
Electrician	2,900– 3,000	2	H. S. Grad.	H. S. 1 Yr.	½ Year
Radio mechanic	2,900– 3,000	2	H. S. Grad.	Not Desig.	--
Mason	2,900– 3,000	2	H. S. 3 Yr.	H. S. Grad.	--
Cashier	2,900– 3,000	2	College	H. S. Grad.	1 Year
Private school teacher	2,900– 3,000	3	College	College	--
Accountant	2,900– 3,000	3	H. S. Grad.	H. S. 3 Yr.	--
Free-lance writer	2,900– 3,000	4	H. S. Grad.	College	1 Year

PART II

CHAPTER III

PROBLEMS EMERGING FROM THE INTERVIEWS WITH THE 75 FAMILIES

By personal interviews with the 75 families selected according to the criteria discussed in Chapter II, 126 problems were collected. These 126 problems have been arranged, as shown in Table 6, in order of total frequency for the three income levels. The problems are numbered from 1 to 126, number 1 referring to the problem emerging most frequently from the interviews and number 126 to the problem raised the least number of times.

The 126 problems fall under nine topic headings chosen according to the nature of the problems. A jury of two professors and two graduate students who checked the problems for topic placement found that many of them, because of their general nature, could be placed under two or more headings. Thus, for example, problem 94 which is related to both children and health might have been placed under topic 4, Health and Recreation, as well as under topic 5, Children and Education, where it was placed by a majority of the jury. Every case where the jury disagreed on the placement of the problems has been indicated in the chapter in which the problem was discussed and a cross reference made to it in the alternate topic. The topic placement has been indicated in parentheses after each problem in Table 6.

These 126 problems are discussed in the nine following chapters by topic divisions so that one may see the number of problems emerging not only from income levels but also from families of varying sizes and occupational groups within these incomes.

Table 6 shows that the 126 problems occur 3,878 times among the 75 families, making an average of 51 problems for each family regardless of income. The 25 families on the income range $900-$1,600 raise these 126 problems 1,002 times, or 25 per cent of the total number of times that they occur. This makes an average of

TABLE 6

PROBLEMS EMERGING FROM PERSONAL INTERVIEWS WITH 75 FAMILIES ARRANGED IN ORDER OF FREQUENCY

Men and Women with Incomes from $900 to $3,000 Wanted to Know:	*Number of Families on Each Income Level Raising the Problem*			*Total Number of Families Raising the Problem*
	$900 to $1,600	*$1,600 to $2,300*	*$2,300 to $3,000*	
1. More about the nutritive value of food and its relation to the cost (Topic 1: Food and Food Buying)	22	20	19	61
2. Where parents could obtain aid in placing their children in better paying positions than their own (Topic 5: Children and Education)	19	20	22	61
3. What is causing the present business depression (Topic 8: General Economic Problems)	19	20	21	60
4. Why knowledge of birth control, for both social and economic reasons, should not be more easily obtainable. (Hygienic aspects as well as economic.) (Topic 4: Health and Recreation)	20	23	17	60
5. Why food prices fluctuate so much more than prices of other household commodities (Topic 9: General Problems in Household Buying)	19	20	20	59
6. What constructive work is being done to equalize wages and cost of living; if employers should not feel greater responsibility for increasing wages when living costs increase (Topic 7: Wages and Employment)	18	20	19	57
7. More about tenant rights under a lease (Topic 3: Housing and Equipment)	18	17	19	54
8. If there is any way for a tenant to get redress without great expense if the terms of the lease are not followed (Topic 3: Housing and Equipment)	18	17	19	54
9. What is the basis for determining rents (Topic 3: Housing and Equipment)	18	17	19	54
10. Why the rich should not be taxed more heavily to secure more nearly equal distribution of incomes and opportunity (Topic 8: General Economic Problems)	20	19	15	54

TABLE 6 (*Continued*)

Men and Women with Incomes from $900 to $3,000 Wanted to Know:	*Number of Families on Each Income Level Raising the Problem*			*Total Number of Families Raising the Problem*
	$900 to $1,600	*$1,600 to $2,300*	*$2,300 to $3,000*	
11. What quantities of food to buy in order to save money (Topic 1: Food and Food Buying)	20	18	15	53
12. What institutions or agencies are making a direct contribution to the household (Topic 3: Housing and Equipment)	17	18	18	53
13. More about the quality of hosiery from the label (Topic 2: Clothing)	10	20	22	52
14. Why poverty must exist; why there is not a more nearly equal distribution of money (Topic 8: General Economic Problems)	17	15	19	51
15. What is the basis for determining premiums for insurance (Topic 6: Insurance and Investments)	14	19	18	51
16. How much insurance one should carry on a given income (Topic 6: Insurance and Investments)	17	16	18	51
17. If parents are not justified in requiring their children who still live with them after beginning to earn money to pay for room and board (Topic 5: Children and Education)	10	20	21	51
18. What to substitute for meat in order to save money and obtain the same nutritive value (Topic 1: Food and Food Buying)	21	16	14	51
19. Why the United States is called such a prosperous country when there is so much poverty and unemployment (Topic 8: General Economic Problems)	17	15	19	51
20. More about European forms of social insurance (Topic 6: Insurance and Investments)	19	16	15	50
21. Where to obtain non-technical information on food values of use in buying, and in planning menus (Topic 1: Food and Food Buying)	10	18	22	50
22. More about the relative wearing qualities of materials used for underwear (Topic 2: Clothing)	7	19	23	49

TABLE 6 (*Continued*)

Men and Women with Incomes from $900 to $3,000 Wanted to Know:	*Number of Families on Each Income Level Raising the Problem*			*Total Number of Families Raising the Problem*
	$900 to $1,600	*$1,600 to $2,300*	*$2,300 to $3,000*	
23. How much reliance to place in nationally advertised hosiery .... (Topic 2: Clothing)	6	20	22	48
24. The proper proportion of money to spend for food .... (Topic 1: Food and Food Buying)	5	18	24	47
25. How to judge the proportion of edible to non-edible food and its relation to the cost (Topic 1: Food and Food Buying)	20	17	10	47
26. Where one could get information about the various terms used for hosiery (service, sheer, etc.). .... (Topic 2: Clothing)	4	20	22	46
27. How to take advantage of sales, and if there is a saving of money in the initial cost at the expense of quality .... (Topic 9: General Problems in Household Buying)	19	17	10	46
28. What are the federal and state regulations for foods .... (Topic 1: Food and Food Buying)	6	18	22	46
29. More about the economics of installment buying .... (Topic 9: General Problems in Household Buying)	17	12	16	45
30. More about the difference between food bought in bulk and food bought in packages (Topic 1: Food and Food Buying)	6	17	22	45
31. What local control the Department of Health exerts over food stores. Relationship between prices of the goods and the higher standards of the stores .... (Topic 1: Food and Food Buying)	12	16	16	44
32. How much of one's income one is justified in paying for rent .... (Topic 3: Housing and Equipment)	6	19	19	44
33. What type or types of insurance are the best investment for one with a limited income .... (Topic 6: Insurance and Investments)	10	16	18	44

TABLE 6 (*Continued*)

Men and Women with Incomes from $900 to $3,000 Wanted to Know:	*Number of Families on Each Income Level Raising the Problem*			*Total Number of Families Raising the Problem*
	$900 to $1,600	*$1,600 to $2,300*	*$2,300 to $3,000*	
34. Whether one can tell definitely how much machinery is causing unemployment by displacing men .... (Topic 8: General Economic Problems)	15	14	14	43
35. How present inheritance laws could be changed to produce a more nearly equal distribution of money .... (Topic 8: General Economic Problems)	18	14	10	42
36. The significance of the different types of markets .... (Topic 9: General Problems in Household Buying)	10	22	9	41
37. How the consumer can be sure that the dealer is selling a good grade of food commodities, such as meat.................. (Topic 1: Food and Food Buying)	6	18	17	41
38. If one is justified in borrowing on one's insurance policy for other than necessities .. (Topic 9: General Problems in Household Buying)	12	14	14	40
39. Why certain stores can offer cut rates, and the effect on other stores .... (Topic 8: General Economic Problems)	10	15	15	40
40. What is the method of financing a coöperative apartment .... (Topic 3: Housing and Equipment)	10	14	15	39
41. How parents could prevent children from leaving school as soon as possible to work; and if their remaining in school longer would not make for greater prosperity ... (Topic 5: Children and Education)	9	14	16	39
42. Varieties of food on the market .... (Topic 1: Food and Food Buying)	7	12	19	38
43. Why labels do not tell the consumer what she needs to know (use, quality, amount, etc.) .... (Topic 9: General Problems in Household Buying)	10	14	14	38
44. When foods are in season, such as fresh fruits and vegetables.................. (Topic 1: Food and Food Buying)	8	13	16	37

TABLE 6 (*Continued*)

Men and Women with Incomes from $900 to $3,000 Wanted to Know:	*Number of Families on Each Income Level Raising the Problem*			*Total Number of Families Raising the Problem*
	$900 to $1,600	*$1,600 to $2,300*	*$2,300 to $3,000*	
45. Why public employment bureaus are so inadequate (Topic 7: Wages and Employment)	14	10	13	37
46. How to judge durability of textile materials (Topic 2: Clothing)	16	10	10	36
47. Comparative prices and food values of fresh, dried, and canned fruits (Topic 1: Food and Food Buying)	8	14	13	35
48. The possibilities of reducing food costs through coöperative buying (Topic 1: Foods and Food Buying)	5	10	20	35
49. Where to obtain information about weights and measures (Topic 9: General Problems in Household Buying)	7	12	16	35
50. Proper proportion of the income to spend for clothes (Topic 2: Clothing)	0	17	18	35
51. How much extensive advertising of a food product affects its price (Topic 1: Food and Food Buying)	1	10	23	34
52. How much a brand name insures a standardized quality of goods (Topic 9: General Problems in Household Buying)	2	16	15	33
53. If recipes and household suggestions in newspapers and magazines are reliable; if they are not for people of means (Topic 1: Food and Food Buying)	6	10	17	33
54. What are the chief sources of the important foods, and how the source influences quality and price (Topic 1: Food and Food Buying)	7	6	20	33
55. Which cuts of meat are most economical, considering price, nutritive value, and amount of fuel needed to cook them (Topic 1: Food and Food Buying)	12	10	11	33
56. The relation between nutritive values and prices of raw, evaporated, and condensed milk (Topic 1: Food and Food Buying)	12	10	11	33

TABLE 6 (*Continued*)

Men and Women with Incomes from $900 to $3,000 Wanted to Know:	*Number of Families on Each Income Level Raising the Problem*			*Total Number of Families Raising the Problem*
	$900 to $1,600	*$1,600 to $2,300*	*$2,300 to $3,000*	
57. What justification there is for the lower wages of women (Topic 7: Wages and Employment)	12	9	11	32
58. More about the relation between school laws and child labor laws (Topic 5: Children and Education)	15	10	7	32
59. How a tariff affects food prices (Topic 8: General Economic Problems)	8	7	16	31
60. More about the original cost of food bought in the market and its cost when ready for consumption (Topic 1: Food and Food Buying)	6	12	13	31
61. How much actual saving there is in the home preparation of food; for example, bread (Topic 9: General Problems in Household Buying)	8	12	11	31
62. How much the practice of exchange and return of textile goods affects prices (Topic 2: Clothing)	3	10	18	31
63. The relative food values of meat and fish, and the cause for such a difference in cost (Topic 1: Food and Food Buying)	8	12	10	30
64. Why the labels on canned fruits and vegetables do not tell more about the contents (Topic 1: Food and Food Buying)	2	10	18	30
65. Whether it would not lower food prices to buy direct from the producer (Topic 9: General Problems in Household Buying)	0	12	18	30
66. More about the keeping qualities of food and their relation to the amount to buy (Topic 1: Food and Food Buying)	7	10	12	29
67. How to determine what are efficient household utensils (Topic 3: Housing and Equipment)	10	9	10	29
68. Why the worker should not be allowed to spend money for alcoholic drinks when he does not drink immoderately (Topic 4: Health and Recreation)	12	7	10	29
69. What is a woman's time in the home worth (Topic 8: General Economic Problems)	7	9	12	28

TABLE 6 (*Continued*)

Men and Women with Incomes from $900 to $3,000 Wanted to Know:	*Number of Families on Each Income Level Raising the Problem*			*Total Number of Families Raising the Problem*
	$900 to $1,600	*$1,600 to $2,300*	*$2,300 to $3,000*	
70. What general connection exists between the terms—tariff, monopoly, public utilities—and the individual household .... (Topic 8: General Economic Problems)	7	8	12	27
71. More about the various sizes of canned goods (Topic 1: Food and Food Buying)	7	10	10	27
72. More about the relationship of price and quality .... (Topic 8: General Economic Problems)	8	10	9	27
73. If it is possible for the consumer to get better style and quality at lower prices ... (Topic 9: General Problems in Household Buying)	7	6	14	27
74. More about the public health resources available to those who cannot afford full medical costs .... (Topic 4: Health and Recreation)	10	9	7	26
75. More about the economics of having clothes cleaned professionally .... (Topic 2: Clothing)	2	10	14	26
76. More about the different brands of canned goods on the market .... (Topic 1: Food and Food Buying)	4	8	14	26
77. Whether home sewing is an economy in the long run if what one might earn otherwise is considered .... (Topic 2: Clothing)	8	8	10	26
78. Whether trading at one satisfactory store would tend to eliminate competition and affect food prices .... (Topic 9: General Problems in Household Buying)	2	8	16	26
79. More about the proportion of money to spend for outside clothes, underwear, shoes, etc. .... (Topic 2: Clothing)	4	10	11	25
80. More about the present regulation for grading food products .... (Topic 1: Food and Food Buying)	4	8	13	25
81. How to identify the chief fabrics sold by the yard .... (Topic 2: Clothing)	4	10	10	24

TABLE 6 (*Continued*)

Men and Women with Incomes from $900 to $3,000 Wanted to Know:	*Number of Families on Each Income Level Raising the Problem*			*Total Number of Families Raising the Problem*
	$900 to $1,600	*$1,600 to $2,300*	*$2,300 to $3,000*	
82. The effects of cold storage on the price of food .... (Topic 1: Food and Food Buying)	10	7	6	23
83. If the equipping of a kitchen from a five-and-ten-cent store does not cost more in the end .... (Topic 3: Housing and Equipment)	7	6	10	23
84. What is the distinction between old age insurance and old age pension .... (Topic 6: Insurance and Investments)	5	9	8	22
85. What is the effect on food prices of paying cash or obtaining credit .... (Topic 8: General Economic Problems)	4	8	10	22
86. How to make comparable figures of the cost of living in Manhattan and in a suburb (Topic 3: Housing and Equipment)	0	8	14	22
87. What effect has the extensive sale of accessories on the employment situation, prices, etc. .... (Topic 8: General Economic Problems)	0	10	11	21
88. The effect of cold storage on the nutritive value of food .... (Topic 1: Food and Food Buying)	8	7	9	24
89. What causes fluctuations in prices in general (Topic 8: General Economic Problems)	4	8	9	21
90. Arguments for and against husbands and wives sharing equally in household expenses. (On the wife's working full or part time) .... (Topic 8: General Economic Problems)	4	6	11	21
91. How can one plan to buy systematically if income is uncertain; if there should not be unemployment insurance to prevent haphazard buying .... (Topic 7: Wages and Employment)	5	9	7	21
92. What is meant by public revenues; how they are obtained, and the relations they bear to free parks, etc. .... (Topic 8: General Economic Problems)	9	5	7	21
93. More about the organization of the Stock Exchange .... (Topic 8: General Economic Problems)	1	8	12	21

TABLE 6 (*Continued*)

Men and Women with Incomes from $900 to $3,000 Wanted to Know:	*Number of Families on Each Income Level Raising the Problem*			*Total Number of Families Raising the Problem*
	$900 to $1,600	*$1,600 to $2,300*	*$2,300 to $3,000*	
94. How schools can afford to give children so much in the way of free clinics (Topic 5: Children and Education)	7	8	5	20
95. If overspecialization is not one of the great difficulties in the way of a skilled laborer's finding employment in the present business depression (Topic 7: Wages and Employment)	2	7	10	19
96. Arguments why women should carry insurance (Topic 6: Insurance and Investments)	8	7	4	19
97. What are the distinctions between speculation, gambling, and investments (Topic 6: Insurance and Investments)	4	8	7	19
98. More about housing conditions and health (Topic 3: Housing and Equipment)	3	7	8	18
99. More about the influence various sizes of cooking utensils have on the amount of fuel consumed (Topic 3: Housing and Equipment)	4	7	6	17
100. What is meant by household capital goods (Topic 8: General Economic Problems)	7	4	6	17
101. Whether an adequate old age pension system would not be a good investment of public funds (Topic 6: Insurance and Investments)	6	4	7	17
102. How the publication of food prices in newspapers affects the consumer (Topic 1: Food and Food Buying)	3	7	6	16
103. Whether the efficient functioning of the Farm Board will result in a radical lowering of food costs (Topic 8: General Economic Problems)	2	6	7	15
104. The relation between cold storage and food distribution (Topic 1: Food and Food Buying)	0	8	7	15
105. Whether groups of people who adhere closely to racial customs buy in large enough quantities to influence market distribution. (Example: the Italians who demand imported cheese and sauces.) (Topic 1: Food and Food Buying)	6	4	5	15

TABLE 6 (*Continued*)

Men and Women with Incomes from $900 to $3,000 Wanted to Know:	*Number of Families on Each Income Level Raising the Problem*			*Total Number of Families Raising the Problem*
	$900 to $1,600	*$1,600 to $2,300*	*$2,300 to $3,000*	
106. What justification stores have for charging more in certain sections of the city even though rents may be similar in the various sections (Topic 8: General Economic Problems)	2	7	5	14
107. More about the prices and the wearing qualities of furs (Topic 2: Clothing)	1	7	6	14
108. Whether there is not some way to provide medical service at lower cost for those in moderate circumstances (Topic 4: Health and Recreation)	1	3	9	13
109. How mass production and standardization of articles, such as felt hats, affects the price (Topic 8: General Economic Problems)	0	6	7	13
110. What is meant by the purchasing power of the dollar. What is meant by the changing value of the dollar (Topic 8: General Economic Problems)	2	3	8	13
111. How to buy ready-to-serve food so as to get the most for the money (Topic 1: Food and Food Buying)	0	7	5	12
112. If there would be any radical lowering of prices if women's clothes were as standardized as men's are (Topic 8: General Economic Problems)	2	5	4	11
113. If one should live in what seems an undesirable neighborhood in order to maintain an insurance policy (Topic 6: Insurance and Investments)	4	3	3	10
114. If employment conditions could not be shown on the label so the consumer might have a chance to buy only goods made under the best conditions (Topic 9: General Problems in Household Buying)	7	2	0	9
115. Why schools do not give more information that will help children to make a better living (that is, higher wages) (Topic 5: Children and Education)	2	1	5	8

TABLE 6 (*Continued*)

Men and Women with Incomes from $900 to $3,000 Wanted to Know:	*Number of Families on Each Income Level Raising the Problem*			*Total Number of Families Raising the Problem*
	$900 to $1,600	*$1,600 to $2,300*	*$2,300 to $3,000*	
116. Why parents are always being asked to contribute to various school enterprises when schools are supposed to be free ..... (Topic 5: Children and Education)	2	1	5	8
117. What effect the present restriction of immigration will have on the labor market eventually .... (Topic 8: General Economic Problems)	2	4	2	8
118. Why schools do not teach children to use leisure time in a more constructive way (Criticism of children's attitude toward school and holidays) .... (Topic 5: Children and Education)	3	2	2	7
119. More about the economic relation between a shorter working week and increased leisure; and if the increased leisure would not cost the working man more, because of greater opportunity to acquire more expensive habits .... (Topic 8: General Economic Problems)	1	2	3	6
120. In what ways the city zoning laws directly affect the individual families .... (Topic 3: Housing and Equipment)	2	3	1	6
121. How much money one is justified in spending for amusement when the necessary food and clothing take practically all of one's money .... (Topic 4: Health and Recreation)	3	1	1	5
122. How far competition regulates prices and wages; how far monopolistic control regulates them .... (Topic 8: General Economic Problems)	2	1	1	4
123. How can the capitalist class justify the statement that the United States offers equal opportunities .... (Topic 8: General Economic Problems)	2	1	1	4
124. If there is any possibility that milk will, like gas, be declared a public utility .... (Topic 8: General Economic Problems)	2	1	0	3
125. Whether consumers' clubs as advocated by Chase and Schlink will ever be developed in a practical way .... (Topic 8: General Economic Problems)	2	1	0	3

TABLE 6 (*Continued*)

Men and Women with Incomes from $900 to $3,000 Wanted to Know:	*Number of Families on Each Income Level Raising the Problem*			*Total Number of Families Raising the Problem*
	$900 to $1,600	*$1,600 to $2,300*	*$2,300 to $3,000*	
126. What is meant by the saying that the prosperity of the country depends upon the inequality of incomes, since this makes for greater capital accumulation .... (Topic : General Economic Problems)	2	0	0	2
Number of times problems were raised by families on each income level	1,002	1,354	1,522	3,878
Per cent of number of times problems were raised by families on each income level	25.8%	34.64%	39.01%	100%
Average number of problems raised by families on each income level	40	54.1	60	51.3

40 problems for each of the 25 families. The 25 families on the $1,600-$2,300 range raise the 126 problems 1,354 times, or 34 per cent of the times they appear. The average is 54 problems per family. On the highest income range, $2,300-$3,000, the problems occur 1,522 times, or 39 per cent of the total number of times that they emerge during the interviews. These 25 families average 60 problems per family. This indicates that as the income increases the families are interested in a wider range of problems or that more families express the same problems more often.

Questions Not Raised by Income Level Group Designated

$900-$1,600

50. Proper proportion of the income to spend for clothes. (2)
65. Whether it would not lower food prices to buy direct from the producer. (9)
86. How to make comparable figures between cost of living in Manhattan and in a suburb. (3)
87. What effect has the extensive sale of accessories on the employment situation, prices, etc. (8)
104. Relation between cold storage and food distribution. (1)
109. How mass production and standardization of articles like felt hats affect the price. (8)

111. How to buy ready-to-serve foods so as to get the most for your money. (1)
124. If there is any possibility that milk will ever be declared a public utility as is gas. (8)

$1,600-$2,300

126. What is meant by the saying that the prosperity of the country depends upon the inequality of incomes since this makes for greater capital accumulation. (8)

$2,300-$3,000

114. If there could not be some way of showing on the label the employment conditions, so giving the consumer a chance to buy only goods made under the best conditions. (8)
125. Consumers' clubs. (8)
126. What is meant by the saying that the prosperity of the country depends upon the inequality of incomes since this makes for greater capital accumulation. (8)

TABLE 7

NUMBER AND PER CENT OF PROBLEMS IN EACH TOPIC RAISED BY THE 75 FAMILIES

TOPIC	*Total Number of Problems in Each Topic*	*Per Cent of 126 Problems in Each Topic*	*Number of Problems in Each Topic Raised by the 75 Families on the Three Income Levels*		
			$900 to $1,600	*$1,600 to $2,300*	*$2,300 to $3,000*
1. Food and Food Buying	32	25.4%	30	32	32
2. Clothing	12	9.5	11	12	12
3. Housing and Equipment	12	9.5	11	12	12
4. Health and Recreation	5	3.9	5	5	5
5. Children and Education	8	6.3	8	8	8
6. Insurance and Investments	9	7.1	9	9	9
7. Wages and Employment	5	3.9	5	5	5
8. General Economic Problems	30	23.8	27	29	28
9. General Problems in Household Buying	13	10.3	12	13	12
	126	100 %	118	125	123

Table 7 shows the number and per cent of the 126 problems falling in each of the 9 topic divisions. Thus, for example, Topic 1 has 32 problems directly relating to food, or 25 per cent of all the problems emerging from the interviews. When one considers that Topic 9, General Problems in Household Buying, includes 13 problems which are so general in nature that they relate to the topic of food as well as to the topics dealing with clothing, house furnishings, and health or recreation, one finds that there is more interest shown in Topic 1 than in any of the other topics.

Table 7 shows that none of the 25 families on each income level raises the entire 126 problems. Each problem omitted by all the families in each income level is listed directly after this table, with the topic placement in parentheses. The families on the lowest income level omit 8 of the 126 problems; those families on the middle income level, only 1; and those on the highest level, 3. One finds that problem 126 is omitted by all the families of two income groups. It was raised on the lowest income group by only two families whose principal wage-earners were communists, and probably emerged because of their political affiliation with the organization rather than for any other reason.

Summary

Personal interviews with 75 families resulted in the emergence of 126 problems. These problems have been arranged in Table 6 according to the frequency with which they occur for the entire income range from $900 to $3,000. A jury checked these problems for placement in nine topic divisions which are to be discussed in more detail in the following chapters. From Table 7 one finds that the problems on food are raised more times than any other problems. Of the families on the three income levels, those on the lowest raised not only fewer problems, but also raised these problems fewer times.

CHAPTER IV

PROBLEMS ON FOOD

The 32 problems relating to food are discussed in this chapter according to the number of problems raised by the 25 families on each of the three income levels, the number of problems raised by the various occupational groups, and the number of problems raised by families of different sizes.

Table 8 gives the 32 problems on food emerging from the interviews. These are numbered the same as in Table 6, page 14, so that one may get some idea of their relative position in the list of 126 problems. These 32 problems occurred 1,096 times during the interviews with the 75 families. The 25 families on the lowest income level, $900-$1,600, raised them 259 times, or 23 per cent of the total number of times that they occur. The 25 families on the two higher income levels raised them 381 and 456 times each, or 34 and 41 per cent, respectively, of the occurrences. These data indicate that as income increases there tends to be an increase in interest in these problems.

Table 9 shows the average number of problems on foods by income levels and occupational groups and gives a total for the occupational groups regardless of the income. We find that among the 25 families on the income level ranging from $900 to $1,600 there are 5 whose principal wage-earners are engaged in the professional occupations. These families raised problems on food 69 times, making an average of 13.8 problems for each of the families. The commercial and industrial groups average 9 problems for each family. The average of the 25 families is 10 problems. The average number of problems for families in each occupation on the various income levels increases as the income increases.

The 20 families in the professional group average 17 problems for each family on the income range of $900-$3,000. This number exceeds the averages for the commercial and industrial groups, which are 13 problems for each group. The average for the 75 families is 14 problems.

TABLE 8

PROBLEMS ON FOOD EMERGING FROM THE INTERVIEWS WITH THE 75 FAMILIES

Men and Women with Incomes from $900 to $3,000 Wanted to Know:	*Number of Families on Each Income Level Raising the Problem*			*Total Number of Families Raising the Problem*
	$900 to $1,600	*$1,600 to $2,300*	*$2,300 to $3,000*	
1. More about the nutritive value of food and its relation to the cost	22	20	19	61
11. What quantities of food to buy in order to save money	20	18	15	53
18. What to substitute for meat in order to save money and obtain the same nutritive value	21	16	14	51
21. Where to obtain non-technical information on food values that will be of use in buying, and in planning menus	10	18	22	50
24. The proper proportion of money to spend for food	5	18	24	47
25. How to judge the proportion of edible to non-edible food and its relation to the cost	20	17	10	47
28. What are the federal and state regulations for foods	6	18	22	46
30. More about the difference between food bought in bulk and food bought in packages	6	17	22	45
31. What local control the Department of Health exerts over the food stores; and what relationship exists between prices of the goods and the higher standards of the stores	12	16	16	44
37. How the consumer can be sure that the dealer is selling a good grade of food commodities such as meat	6	18	17	41
42. Varieties of food on the market	7	12	19	38
44. When foods are in season, such as fresh fruits and vegetables	8	13	16	37
47. Comparative prices and food values of fresh, dried, and canned fruits	8	14	13	35
48. The possibilities of reducing food costs through coöperative buying	5	10	20	35
51. How much extensive advertising of a food product affects its price	1	10	23	34
53. If recipes and household suggestions in newspapers and magazines are reliable; if they are not for people of means	6	10	17	33
54. What are the chief sources of the important foods, and how the source influences quality and price	7	6	20	33

TABLE 8 (*Continued*)

Men and Women with Incomes from $900 to $3,000 Wanted to Know:		*Number of Families on Each Income Level Raising the Problem*			*Total Number of Families Raising the Problem*
		$900 to $1,600	*$1,600 to $2,300*	*$2,300 to $3,000*	
55. Which cuts of meat are most economical, considering price, nutritive value, and amount of fuel needed to prepare them . .		12	10	11	33
56. The relation between nutritive values and prices of raw, evaporated, and condensed milk		12	10	11	33
60. More about the original cost of food bought in the market and its cost when ready for consumption		6	12	13	31
63. The relative food values of meat and fish, and the cause for such a difference in price		8	12	10	30
64. Why the labels on canned fruits and vegetables do not tell more about the contents		2	10	18	30
66. More about the keeping qualities of food and their relation to the amount to buy . .		7	10	12	29
71. More about the various sizes of canned goods		7	10	12	29
76. More about the different brands of canned goods on the market		4	18	14	36
80. More about the present regulations for grading food products		4	8	13	25
82. The effects of cold storage on the price of food		10	7	6	23
88. The effect of cold storage on the nutritive value of food		8	7	6	21
102. How the publication of food prices in newspapers affects the consumer		3	7	6	16
104. The relation between cold storage and food distribution and costs		0	8	7	15
105. Whether groups who adhere closely to racial customs buy in large enough quantities to influence market distribution; for example, the Italians who import cheese and sauces		6	4	5	15
111. How to buy ready-to-serve foods so as to get the most for the money		0	7	5	12
Total Number of problems—32	Number of times problems were raised by families on each income level	259	381	456	1,096

TABLE 8 (*Continued*)

Men and Women with Incomes from $900 to $3,000 Wanted to Know:		*Number of Families on Each Income Level Raising the Problem* $900 to $1,600	$1,600 to $2,300	$2,300 to $3,000	*Total Number of Families Raising the Problem*
25.4% of the 126 problems	Per cent of number of times problems were raised by families on each income level	23.6%	34.7%	41.6%	100%
	Average number of problems raised by families on each income level	10.3	15.2	18.2	14.6

TABLE 9

NUMBER OF PROBLEMS ON FOOD BY INCOME LEVELS AND OCCUPATIONAL GROUPS

Distribution of Occupations on Various Income Levels	*Number of Families in Each Occupational Group*		*Number of Times Problems Were Raised by Each Occupational Group*		*Average Number of Problems Raised per Family in Each Occupational Group**	
$900–$1,600						
Professional	5		69		13.8	
Commercial	7		65		9.2	
Industrial	13		125		9.6	
Total		25		259		10.3
$1,600–$2,300						
Professional	7		125		17.8	
Commercial	8		114		14.2	
Industrial	10		142		14.2	
Total		25		381		15.2
$2,300–$3,000						
Professional	8		157		19.6	
Commercial	10		169		16.9	
Industrial	7		130		18.5	
Total		25		456		18.2
Total of the Income Ranges		75		1,096		14.6
Professional	20		351		17.5	
Commercial	25		348		13.9	
Industrial	30		397		13.2	

* Column 3 is obtained by dividing column 2 by column 1.

Table 9 shows, as does the preceding table, that there is an increase of interest in these problems as the income increases. In addition we find that the professional families average more problems per family than either of the other two occupational groups.

Table 9 shows the frequency with which problems occur by occupational groups on the different income levels, but does not indicate the distribution of the problems among these groups. Table 10 gives the number of problems raised by the group; and then in

TABLE 10

DISTRIBUTION OF THE 32 PROBLEMS ON FOOD AMONG THE INCOME LEVELS AND OCCUPATIONAL GROUPS

Distribution of Occupations on Various Income Levels	*Total Number of Families*	*Total Number of Problems Raised by the Group*	*Numbers of the Problems Not Raised (See Table 8)*
$900–$1,600			
Professional	5	29	51, 104, 111
Commercial	7	24	48, 51, 63, 64, 80, 104, 111
Industrial	13	27	64, 76, 102, 104, 111
$1,600–$2,300			
Professional	7	32	--
Commercial	8	30	80, 105
Industrial	10	32	--
$2,300–$3,000			
Professional	8	31	51
Commercial	10	32	--
Industrial	7	26	25, 82, 88, 102, 104, 105

the last column the numbers of the problems not raised by any families within the group, in order to show those problems which seem to be of no interest. For example, one finds that none of the families of the income range of $900-$1,600 raise problems 104 and 111, which deal with the relation between cold storage and food distribution and with the buying of ready-to-serve foods so as to get the most for the money expended. The interviewer found that the buying of ready-cooked food was an almost unheard-of luxury among the families on this income, who used little food, except baker's bread, that had been prepared outside the home.

There is no problem which is omitted by all of any one occupa-

TABLE 11

NUMBER OF PROBLEMS ON FOOD RAISED BY FAMILIES OF DIFFERENT SIZES AND INCOME LEVELS

Income Range and Number of Children in the Family	*Number of Families*	*Number of Problems Raised by the Families*	*Average Number of Problems per Family**
$900–$1,200			
2 children	2	27	13.5
3 children	1	7	7
4 children	--	--	--
Total	3	34	11.3
$1,200–$1,500			
2 children	9	94	10.5
3 children	6	56	9.3
4 children	--	--	--
Total	15	150	10.0
$1,500–$1,800			
2 children	6	77	12.4
3 children	5	65	13.0
4 children	2	23	11.5
Total	13	165	12.5
$1,800–$2,100			
2 children	6	97	16.1
3 children	4	63	15.6
4 children	1	11	11.0
Total	11	171	15.5
$2,100–$2.400			
2 children	5	68	13.6
3 children	2	38	19.0
4 children	1	14	14.0
Total	8	120	15.0
$2,400–$2,700			
2 children	5	87	17.4
3 children	4	75	18.7
4 children	2	35	17.5
Total	11	197	24.6
$2,700–$3,000			
2 children	10	173	17.3
3 children	3	62	20.6
4 children	1	24	24.0
Total	14	259	18.5
$900–$3,000			
2 children	43	623	14.4
3 children	25	366	14.6
4 children	7	107	15.3
Total	75	1,096	14.6

* Column 3 is obtained by dividing column 2 by column 1.

tional group on the three income levels. Of the 32 problems on the topic of food that emerge from the interviews with the 75 families, 19 are of sufficient interest to be raised by each occupational group and the other 13 emerge in interviews with some families and fail to emerge with others.

Table 11 gives the number of problems raised by families of different sizes and incomes. Among the 75 families there are 43 families with 2 children. These families average 14 problems each. This average corresponds with the averages of the families with 3 and 4 children. The size of the family, therefore, does not seem to determine the amount of interest in the problems raised on the topic of food. In the income range of $2,700-$3,000 there is one family with 4 children. The principal wage-earner is a writer and many of the problems that he and his wife raised were due to their interest in many phases of the topic. The fact that they raised so many problems increases the average for this income level, and so makes the difference due to size of family appear greater than it really is. The table also shows the same fact as the preceding tables —that as income increases there is an increase in the number of problems per family.

Summary

1. The 32 problems on the topic relating to problems on food occur 1,096 times among the 75 families, making an average of 14.6 problems for each of the families regardless of income, occupation, or size of the family.

2. As the income increases there is an increase in the average number of problems per family regardless of occupational distribution.

3. Among the occupational groups the professional families raise more problems than the commercial and industrial groups which average the same number.

4. Families with 2, 3, and 4 children average about the same number of problems.

5. Each of the 75 families raised one or more problems on the topic of food.

6. There are only 2 problems not raised by any of the families on the lower income level. There are 19 problems which are raised by one or more families in each of the income levels and occupational groups.

CHAPTER V

PROBLEMS ON CLOTHING

The 12 problems relating to clothing emerging from the interviews with the 75 families are discussed in this chapter according to the average number of problems on this topic by income levels and occupational groups and then in relation to the size of the family.

Table 12 gives the list of problems on this topic of clothing as taken from the list of 126 problems in Table 6. The same numbering is used here as in that table so that one may have some idea of the position of these problems in relation to the whole group.

Table 12 shows that these 12 problems occurred 412 times during the interviews with the 75 families, making an average of 5.4 times for each of the families. The 25 families on the lowest income level, $900-$1,600, raised them 65 times, or 15 per cent of the total number of times that they occurred during the interviews. This makes an average of over 2 problems for each family. The 25 families on the income range $1,600-$2,300 raised these problems 161 times, or 38 per cent of the total number of times during the 75 interviews. This makes a considerable increase in the average number of times problems occur in this group as there are an average of 6 in contrast to the 2 problems on the lower level. There is not so large an increase on the next income level, as these 25 families raised the 12 problems 186 times, or 45 per cent of the total number of occurrence, making an average of 7 times for each family. The table indicates that as the income increases from the lowest to the middle range there is quite an increase in interest in these problems, since there is an increase from 2 problems per family on the lowest to 6 problems on the next range. The increase is not so great between the middle and highest income ranges as there is only an average increase of one problem per family.

Table 13 shows the distribution of the 25 families on each income level among the three occupational groups. Thus, for example, on the $900-$1,600 income level there are 5 families where the principal wage-earners are engaged in the professional occupa-

TABLE 12

PROBLEMS ON CLOTHING EMERGING FROM THE INTERVIEWS WITH THE 75 FAMILIES

Men and Women with Incomes from $900 to $3,000 Wanted to Know:		*Number of Families on Each Income Level Raising the Problem*			*Total Number of Families Raising the Problem*
		$900 to $1,600	*$1,600 to $2,300*	*$2,300 to $3,000*	
13. More about the quality of hosiery from the label		10	20	22	52
22. More about the relative wearing qualities of materials used for underwear		7	19	23	49
23. How much reliance to place in nationally advertised hosiery		6	20	22	48
26. Where one could get information about the various terms used for hosiery (service, sheer, etc.)		4	20	22	46
46. How to judge durability of textile materials		16	10	10	36
50. Proper proportion of the income to spend for clothes		0	17	18	35
62. How much the practice of exchange and return of textile goods affects prices		3	10	18	31
75. More about the economics of having clothes cleaned professionally		2	10	14	26
77. Whether home sewing is an economy in the long run if what one might earn otherwise is considered		8	8	10	26
79. More about the proportion of money to spend for outside clothes, underwear, shoes, etc.		4	10	11	25
81. How to identify the chief fabrics sold by the yard		4	10	10	24
107. More about the prices and the wearing qualities of furs		1	7	6	14
Total Number of problems—12	Number of times problems were raised by families on each income level	65	161	186	412
9.5% of the 126 problems	Per cent of times problems were raised by families on each income level	15.8%	38.8%	45.1%	100%
	Average number of problems raised by families on each income level	2.6	6.4	7.4	5.4

TABLE 13

NUMBER OF PROBLEMS ON CLOTHING BY INCOME LEVELS AND OCCUPATIONAL GROUPS

Distribution of Occupations on Various Income Levels	*Number of Families in Each Occupational Group*		*Number of Times Problems Were Raised by Each Occupational Group*		*Average Number of Problems Raised per Family in Each Occupational Group**	
$900–$1,600						
Professional	5		21		4.2	
Commercial	7		25		3.5	
Industrial	13		19		1.4	
Total		25		65		2.6
$1,600–$2,300						
Professional	7		54		7.7	
Commercial	8		55		6.8	
Industrial	10		52		5.2	
Total		25		161		6.4
$2,300–$3,000						
Professional	8		71		8.8	
Commercial	10		70		7.0	
Industrial	7		45		6.4	
Total		25		186		7.4
Total of the income ranges						
Professional	20		146		7.3	
Commercial	25		150		6.0	
Industrial	30		116		3.8	
Total		75		412		5.4

* Column 3 is obtained by dividing column 2 by column 1.

tions. These 5 families raise problems on clothing 21 times, making an average of 4.2 problems for each family. The 7 commercial and 13 industrial families raise these problems 25 and 19 times, respectively, making averages of 3.5 and 1.4 problems for each group. As has been shown in Table 13, the average for the 25 families on this income range is 2.6 problems per family. This indicates that among the 25 families the professional families show the most interest in these problems and the industrial families show the least. This is to be expected when one considers the nature of the occupations of the two groups; for example, the wage-earner of the professional class has to impress people by his appearance while the industrial worker often wears a specified uniform.

As the income increases there is an increase in the average number of problems raised by families in each occupational group. While the professional group raises more problems than the other two groups on each income level, the industrial families make the largest increase in the average number of problems since they increase from 1 problem on the lowest level to 6 problems on the highest level.

TABLE 14

Distribution of the 12 Problems on Clothing Among the Income Levels and Occupational Groups

	Total Number of Families	*Total Number of Problems Raised by the Group*	*Numbers of the Problems Not Raised (See Table 12)*
$900–$1,600			
Professional	5	11	50
Commercial	7	10	50, 107
Industrial	13	6	13, 23, 50, 62, 75, 107
$1,600–$2,300			
Professional	7	12	--
Commercial	8	12	--
Industrial	10	12	--
$2,300–$3,000			
Professional	8	12	--
Commercial	10	12	--
Industrial	7	12	--

Table 14 shows the frequency with which problems on clothing were raised by families in the different occupational groups, but it does not indicate whether the same problems occur in all groups or whether there is a wide distribution of problems. The table shows that on the lowest income level problem 50, which relates to the proper proportion of the income to spend for clothes, was not raised by any of the 25 families. The commercial and industrial groups do not raise problem 107, prices and wearing qualities of furs. The industrial group in addition does not raise problems 13, 23, 62 and 75, which are listed in Table 12, page 36. It is interesting, however, that all 12 problems are raised by one or more families within each of the occupational groups on the two upper income levels.

TABLE 15

NUMBER OF PROBLEMS ON CLOTHING RAISED BY FAMILIES OF DIFFERENT SIZES AND INCOME LEVELS

Income Range and Number of Children in the Family	*Number of Families*	*Number of Problems Raised by the Families*	*Average Number of Problems per Family**
$900–$1,200			
2 children	2	8	4
3 children	1	2	2
4 children	--	--	--
Total	3	10	3.3
$1,200–$1,500			
2 children	9	25	2.7
3 children	6	14	2.3
4 children	--	--	--
Total	15	39	2.8
$1,500–$1,800			
2 children	6	32	5.3
3 children	5	20	4.0
4 children	2	2	1.0
Total	13	54	4.1
$1,800–$2,100			
2 children	6	39	6.5
3 children	4	26	6.5
4 children	1	6	6.0
Total	11	71	6.4
$2,100–$2,400			
2 children	5	28	5.6
3 children	2	17	8.5
4 children	1	7	7.0
Total	8	52	6.5
$2,400–$2,700			
2 children	5	35	7.0
3 children	4	24	6.0
4 children	2	9	4.5
Total	11	68	8.5
$2,700–$3,000			
2 children	10	82	8.2
3 children	3	28	9.3
4 children	1	8	8.0
Total	14	118	8.4
$900–$3,000			
2 children	43	249	5.7
3 children	25	131	5.2
4 children	7	32	4.5
Total	75	412	5.4

* Column 3 is obtained by dividing column 2 by column 1.

Table 12 shows the frequency with which these problems occur among the 25 families on the income level, and Table 13 indicates that the professional families raise problems more frequently than the other two occupational groups.

Table 15 shows that there are 12 problems on clothing raised 412 times by the 75 families. This would make an average of 5.4 problems raised per family, irrespective of the size of the family. This average holds true with a slight variation when one notes that families with 2 children raise 5.7 problems per family, families with 3 children raise 5.2 problems, and families with 4 children raise 4.5 problems.

As shown in Table 14, one finds that as the income increases the number of problems tends to increase. Families on income ranges from $2,400 to $2,700 raise about the same number of problems per family. In general, families with 2 and 3 children have more problems than families with 4 children, but the difference is not important. In most families where the children are quite young the clothes are passed on from child to child. This is not true as the children grow older and more conscious of social distinctions.

Summary

1. The problems on clothing emerge 412 times among the 75 families, making an average of 5.4 problems on this topic for each of the families regardless of income, occupation, or size of the family.

2. As the income increases there is an increase in the average number of problems per family regardless of occupational distribution.

3. Among the occupational groups the professional families average 7 problems for each of the 20 families in this group and the commercial and industrial groups 6 and 3 problems, respectively.

4. The size of the family does not seem to make a difference in the average number of problems raised, since families with 2, 3, and 4 children average about the same number of problems.

5. Each of the 75 families raises one or more problems on this topic.

6. Problem 50, which refers to the proper proportion of the income to spend for clothing, was not raised by any families on the $900-$1,600 income level. All the 12 problems on clothing are raised by some families within each of the occupational groups on the two upper income levels.

CHAPTER VI

PROBLEMS ON HOUSING AND EQUIPMENT

The 12 problems relating to housing and equipment emerging from the interviews with the 75 families are discussed in this chapter by income levels and occupational groups and then in relation to the size of the family. They are listed in Table 16. Problem number 98, dealing with housing conditions and health, might have been placed in topic 4, health and recreation, as well as under this heading. Reference is made to problem 98 again in the next chapter.

The same numbering of the problems is used as in the list of 126 problems in Chapter III so as to show their position in relation to the 126 problems.

Table 16 shows that the 75 families raised the 12 problems relating to the topic of housing and equipment 413 times, making an average of 5.5 times for each family. The 25 families on the lowest income level, \$900-\$1,600, raised the problems 113 times, or 27 per cent of the total number of times that they occur. This averages 4.5 problems for each family. The two upper income levels raised the problems 34 and 38 per cent of the total number of times that they occur, which makes an average of 5.6 and 6.3 problems, respectively, for these two income levels. This would indicate that the interest is about the same on the entire income range of \$900-\$1,600, with only a slight increase in the average number of problems as the income increases.

All the families on the highest income level, \$2,300-\$3,000, average more problems per family than those on the two lower income levels. The professional group, as on the other two income levels, leads in the number of problems per family, since these families raise 6.7 problems, while the commercial and industrial families raise 5.9 and 6.4 problems each. The average for the 25 families without regard to occupation is 6.3 problems.

Table 17 indicates that as the income increases there is an increase in the number of problems per family regardless of the occupational distribution. Among the occupations, the professional families tend

TABLE 16

PROBLEMS ON HOUSING AND EQUIPMENT EMERGING FROM THE INTERVIEWS WITH THE 75 FAMILIES

Men and Women with Incomes from $900 to $3,000 Wanted to Know:		*Number of Families on Each Income Level Raising the Problem*			*Total Number of Families Raising the Problem*
		$900 to $1,600	*$1,600 to $2,300*	*$2,300 to $3,000*	
7. More about tenant rights under a lease . .		18	17	19	54
8. If there is any way for a tenant to get redress without great expense if the terms of the lease are not followed		18	17	19	54
9. What is the basis for determining rents . . .		18	17	19	54
12. What institutions or agencies are making a direct contribution to the household		17	18	18	53
32. How much of one's income one is justified in paying for rent		6	19	19	44
40. What is the method of financing a coöperative apartment		10	14	15	39
67. How to determine what are efficient household utensils		10	9	10	29
83. If the equipping of a kitchen from a five-and-ten-cent store does not cost more in the end		7	6	10	23
86. How to make comparable figures of the cost of living in Manhattan and in a suburb . .		0	8	14	22
98. More about housing conditions and health		3	7	8	18
99. More about the influence various sizes of cooking utensils have on the amount of fuel consumed		4	7	6	17
120. In what ways the city zoning laws directly affect the individual families		2	3	1	6
Total number of problems—12	Number of times problems were raised by families on each income level	113	142	158	413
9.5% of the 126 problems	Per cent of number of times problems were raised by 25 families on each income level	27.4	34.4	38.2	100
	Average number of problems raised by 25 families on each income level	4.5	5.6	6.3	5.5

TABLE 17

NUMBER OF PROBLEMS ON HOUSING AND EQUIPMENT BY INCOME LEVELS AND OCCUPATIONAL GROUPS

Distribution of Occupations on Various Income Levels	*Number of Families in Each Occupational Group*		*Number of Times Problems Were Raised by Each Occupational Group*		*Average Number of Problems Raised per Family in Each Occupational Group**	
$900–$1,600						
Professional	5		28		5.6	
Commercial	7		38		5.4	
Industrial	13		47		3.6	
Total		25		113		4.5
$1,600–$2,300						
Professional	7		41		5.8	
Commercial	8		42		5.2	
Industrial	10		59		5.9	
Total		25		142		5.6
$2,300–$3,000						
Professional	8		54		6.7	
Commercial	10		59		5.9	
Industrial	7		45		6.4	
Total		25		158		6.3
Total of the income ranges						
Professional	20		123		6.1	
Commercial	25		139		5.5	
Industrial	30		151		5.0	
Total		75		413		5.5

* Column 3 is obtained by dividing column 2 by column 1.

to raise slightly more problems than the other two occupational groups, both of which raise practically the same number. There is no marked distinction in the number of problems among the occupational groups. This table shows what was brought out in the preceding table, namely, that the interest in these problems does not change with the income; and in addition we may add that the interest seems to be the same in the various occupations.

Table 18 shows the distribution of the 12 problems relating to housing and equipment among the families of different occupations and incomes. This table differs from Table 17 in that it does not show the frequency with which the problems were raised, as does the preceding table. One sees that the 5 professional families on the

TABLE 18

DISTRIBUTION OF THE 12 PROBLEMS ON HOUSING AND EQUIPMENT AMONG THE INCOME LEVELS AND OCCUPATIONAL GROUPS

Distribution of Occupations on Various Income Levels	*Total Number of Families*	*Total Number of Problems Raised by the Group*	*Numbers of the Problems Not Raised (See Table 16)*
$900–$1,600			
Professional	5	11	86
Commercial	7	10	86, 99
Industrial	13	10	86, 120
$1,600–$2,300			
Professional	7	11	83
Commercial	8	12	--
Industrial	10	11	120
$2,300–$3,000			
Professional	8	12	--
Commercial	10	11	120
Industrial	7	11	120

$900-$1,600 income level raise all of the 12 problems on this topic. They omit problem 86 which deals with the making of comparable figures to show cost of living in Manhattan and the suburbs. From observation of their standard of living and the budget necessary to maintain it one can see that the item of carfare in many cases is enough to discourage them from living in a suburb. The table shows that the same problem is omitted by each of the occupational groups on the lowest level. In addition to problem 86, the commercial group omits problem 99 which deals with kitchen equipment, and the industrial group omits number 120 which deals with the relation of zoning laws to the individual families.

Table 18 shows that only four of the 12 problems are entirely omitted by any occupational group. This, of course, does not mean that individual families within the group may not have omitted one or more of the problems. The table also indicates that as the income increases families on each income level raise about the same number of problems.

Table 19 shows that the 75 families raise the 12 problems on the topic of housing and equipment 413 times, making an average of

TABLE 19

NUMBER OF PROBLEMS ON HOUSING AND EQUIPMENT RAISED BY FAMILIES OF DIFFERENT SIZES AND INCOME LEVELS

Income Range and Number of Children in the Family	*Number of Families*	*Number of Problems Raised by the Families*	*Average Number of Problems per Family**
$900–$1,200			
2 children	2	9	4.5
3 children	1	3	3.0
4 children	--	--	--
Total	3	12	4.0
$1,200–$1,500			
2 children	9	38	4.2
3 children	6	25	4.1
4 children	--	--	--
Total	15	63	4.2
$1,500–$1,800			
2 children	6	38	6.3
3 children	5	22	4.4
4 children	2	12	6.0
Total	13	72	5.5
$1,800–$2,100			
2 children	6	29	4.8
3 children	4	23	5.6
4 children	1	7	7.0
Total	11	59	5.3
$2,100–$2,400			
2 children	5	28	5.6
3 children	2	13	6.5
4 children	1	8	8.0
Total	8	49	6.1
$2,400–$2,700			
2 children	5	27	5.4
3 children	4	24	6.0
4 children	2	15	7.5
Total	11	66	6.0
$2,700–$3,000			
2 children	10	58	5.8
3 children	3	23	7.6
4 children	1	11	11.0
Total	14	92	6.5
Total—$900–$3,000			
2 children	43	227	5.2
3 children	25	113	4.5
4 children	7	53	7.5
Total	75	413	5.5

* Column 3 is obtained by dividing column 2 by column 1.

5.5 problems per family. As in the case of topics relating to food and clothing, one finds that as the income increases the number of problems increases, but not to such a marked degree as in the case of the other topics. There is only a slight increase in the average number of problems. However, this table shows that there are more problems raised by the larger families, since families with 2, 3, and 4 children average 5, 4, and 7 problems, respectively.

SUMMARY

1. The 12 problems on the topic relating to housing and equipment occur 413 times among the 75 families, making an average of 5.5 problems for each family regardless of income, occupation, or size of family.

2. As the income increases there is only a slight increase in the average number of problems per family.

3. Among the occupational groups the professional families raise slightly more problems than the other two groups which raise about the same number. However, there is no marked distinction between occupational groups.

4. Among the 12 problems, problem 86 is omitted by all families on the $900-$1,600 income level. Problems 99, 120, and 83 are omitted by one or more occupational groups.

5. The 12 problems are about equally distributed over the three income levels with the exception of problem 86, as noted above.

6. Families with 4 children average more problems per family than families with 2 or 3 children.

7. The number of problems increases progressively in the families with 4 children from the smaller to the larger incomes.

CHAPTER VII

PROBLEMS ON HEALTH AND RECREATION

The 5 problems relating to health and recreation emerging from the interviews with the 75 families are discussed by income levels and occupational groups and then in relation to the size of the family. Table 20 gives the list of problems on this topic as taken from the list of 126 in Chapter III. The same numbering is used as in that chapter so that one may get some idea of their position in relation to the whole group of 126 problems. In addition to the problems listed in this table one finds that problem 98—more about housing conditions and health—might have been placed under this topic as well as under topic 3, housing and equipment, where the majority of the jury placed it; also problem 94—how schools can afford to give so much in the way of free clinics.

Table 20 shows that the 5 problems on the topic of health and recreation occurred 133 times during the interviews with the 75 families. The 25 families on the lowest income level, $900-$1,600, raised them 46 times, or 34 per cent of the total number of times they occur. The 25 families on the two higher income levels raised them 43 and 44 times each, or 32 and 33 per cent, respectively. This indicates that the interest in this topic does not vary with the income. The problem of most general interest related to the subject of birth control. In Chapter II, Table 4, one finds that 61 per cent of these families presumably are not restricted by religion from obtaining knowledge of birth control.

Table 21 shows the average number of problems on health and recreation raised by the three occupational groups on each income level. On the lowest level there are the same number of problems raised as on the higher income levels. Each occupational group shows the same interest as far as the number of problems brought out from the interviews indicates interest.

Table 22 indicates the distribution of problems among the occupational groups on the different income levels, but it does not take into account the frequency with which the problems occur as does

TABLE 20

PROBLEMS ON HEALTH AND RECREATION EMERGING FROM THE INTERVIEWS WITH THE 75 FAMILIES

Men and Women with Incomes from $900 to $3,000 Wanted to Know:		*Number of Families on Each Income Level Raising the Problem*			*Total Number of Families Raising the Problem*
		$900 to $1,600	*$1,600 to $2,300*	*$2,300 to $3,000*	
4. Why knowledge of birth control, for both social and economic reasons, should not be more easily obtainable. (Hygienic aspects as well as economic)		20	23	17	60
68. Why the worker should not be allowed to spend money for alcoholic drinks when he does not drink immoderately		12	7	10	29
74. More about the public health resources available to those who cannot afford full medical costs		10	9	7	26
108. Whether there is not some way to provide medical service at lower cost for those in moderate circumstances		1	3	9	13
121. How much money one is justified in spending for amusement when the necessary food and clothing take practically all of one's money		3	1	1	5
Total Number of Problems—5	Number of times problems were raised by families on each income level	46	43	44	133
3.9% of the 126 problems	Per cent of number of times problems were raised by 25 families on each income level	34.7	32.3	33	100
	Average number of problems raised by 25 families on each income level	1.8	1.7	1.7	1.7

Table 20. One finds that problems 108 and 121, which relate to the cost of medical service and to the amount of money one is justified in spending for recreation, are the only problems not raised by one or more families within each occupational group on each income level.

Table 23 shows the number of problems relating to health and recreation raised by families of different sizes and income. The

TABLE 21

NUMBER OF PROBLEMS ON HEALTH AND RECREATION BY INCOME LEVELS AND OCCUPATIONAL GROUPS

Distribution of Occupations on Various Income Levels	*Number of Families in Each Occupational Group*		*Number of Times Problems Were Raised by Each Occupational Group*		*Average Number of Problems Raised per Family in Each Occupational Group**	
$900–$1,600						
Professional	5		10		2.0	
Commercial	7		13		1.8	
Industrial	13		23		1.7	
Total		25		46		1.8
$1,600–$2,300						
Professional	7		14		2.0	
Commercial	8		10		1.2	
Industrial	10		19		1.9	
Total		25		43		1.7
$2,300–$3,000						
Professional	8		17		2.0	
Commercial	10		15		1.5	
Industrial	7		12		1.7	
Total		25		44		1.7
Total of the income ranges						
Professional	20		41		2.0	
Commercial	25		38		1.5	
Industrial	30		54		1.8	
Total		75		133		1.7

* Column 3 is obtained by dividing column 2 by column 1.

table shows that there is only a slight variation in the number of problems. There is a tendency for the large families to raise more problems, but the difference is not marked. Families with four children raise an average of 2.4 problems, or .8 of a problem more than families with two children whose average is 1.6 problems.

SUMMARY

1. There are 5 problems on the topic of health and recreation which occur 133 times in the interviews with the 75 families. This makes an average of 1.7 problems for each family.

There is one problem listed under the topic of housing and equipment, Chapter VI, which belongs in this chapter as well, since it

TABLE 22

DISTRIBUTION OF THE 5 PROBLEMS ON HEALTH AND RECREATION AMONG THE INCOME LEVELS AND OCCUPATIONAL GROUPS

Distribution of Occupations on Various Income Levels	*Total Number of Families*	*Total Number of Problems Raised by the Group*	*Numbers of the Problems Not Raised (See Table 20)*
$900–$1,600			
Professional	5	3	108, 121
Commercial	7	4	108
Industrial	13	5	--
$1,600–$2,300			
Professional	7	5	--
Commercial	8	4	121
Industrial	10	3	108, 121
$2,300–$3,000			
Professional	8	5	--
Commercial	10	5	--
Industrial	7	4	121

refers to the problem of housing conditions in relation to health; and in Chapter VIII, problem 94, in Table 24, might also be placed under this topic since it refers to children and school clinics.

2. The average number of problems, 1.7, remains the same regardless of occupation, income, or the size of the family.

3. Among the 5 problems there are 3 which are always raised by one or more families within each occupational group and income level. These 3 problems relate to birth control knowledge, prohibition, and medical costs.

TABLE 23

NUMBER OF PROBLEMS ON HEALTH AND RECREATION RAISED BY FAMILIES OF DIFFERENT SIZES AND INCOME LEVELS

Income Range and Number of Children in the Family	*Number of Families*		*Number of Problems Raised by the Families*		*Average Number of Problems per Family**	
$900–$1,200						
2 children	2		4		2	
3 children	1		2		2	
4 children	--		--		--	
Total		3		6		2.0
$1,200–$1,500						
2 children	9		15		1.6	
3 children	6		10		1.6	
4 children	--		--		--	
Total		15		25		1.6
$1,500–$1,800						
2 children	6		10		1.6	
3 children	5		11		2.2	
4 children	2		5		2.5	
Total		13		26		2.0
$1,800–$2,100						
2 children	6		8		1.3	
3 children	4		5		1.2	
4 children	1		2		2.0	
Total		11		15		1.3
$2,100–$2,400						
2 children	5		8		1.6	
3 children	2		6		3.0	
4 children	1		3		3.0	
Total		8		17		2.1
$2,400–$2,700						
2 children	5		9		1.8	
3 children	4		5		1.2	
4 children	2		4		2.0	
Total		11		18		1.6
$2,700–$3,000						
2 children	10		15		1.5	
3 children	3		8		2.6	
4 children	1		3		3.0	
Total		14		26		1.8
Total—$900–$3,000						
2 children	43		69		1.6	
3 children	25		47		1.8	
4 children	7		17		2.4	
Total		75		133		1.7

* Column 3 is obtained by dividing column 2 by column 1.

CHAPTER VIII

PROBLEMS ON CHILDREN AND EDUCATION

The 8 problems relating to children and education are discussed together in this chapter. Several of these problems might have been listed under other topics; for example, number 94 dealing with school clinics might have been placed under the topic of health and recreation, but it seemed best to place it in this division and to make reference to it in the preceding chapter.

Table 24 gives the lists of problems on this topic as taken from the list of 126 in Chapter III. The same numbering is used as in that chapter so that one may get some idea of their position in relation to the whole group of 126 problems.

Table 25 shows the average number of problems on children and education raised by families on different income levels and occupational groups. The table shows the average number of problems raised on each income level by the three occupational groups. On the lowest level there are 25 families whose income is in the range of \$900-\$1,600. Among these 25 families there are 5 whose principal wage-earners are engaged in the professional occupations. This table shows the frequency with which they raised problems on this topic. They raised problems 14 times, making an average of 2.8 problems for each of the 5 families. This average does not differ markedly from the averages for the other occupational groups. There is a tendency for more problems to be raised on the highest income level, \$2,300-\$3,000, but the increase is slight.

Table 26 differs from the preceding table which deals with the frequency with which problems occur on this topic by showing the number of problems which do occur within the income levels and the number of the problems raised by each occupational group. For example, one finds that the 5 professional families on the lowest income level raise all 8 of the problems listed in Table 24. The commercial group of families on the same income level raises 5 of the 8 problems and omits problems 115, 116, and 118. These problems deal with the opinion of some of the parents that the schools

TABLE 24

PROBLEMS ON CHILDREN AND EDUCATION EMERGING FROM PERSONAL INTERVIEWS WITH 75 FAMILIES

	Men and Women with Incomes from $900 to $3,000 Wanted to Know:	*Number of Families on Each Income Level Raising the Problem*			*Total Number of Families Raising the Problem*
		$900 to $1,600	*$1,600 to $2,300*	*$2,300 to $3,000*	
	2. Where parents could obtain aid in placing their children in better paying positions than their own	19	20	22	61
	17. If parents are not justified in requiring their children who still live with them after beginning to earn money to pay for room and board	10	20	21	51
	41. How parents could prevent children from leaving school as soon as possible to work; and if their remaining in school longer would not make for greater prosperity	9	14	16	39
	58. More about the relation between school laws and child labor laws	15	10	7	32
	94. How schools can afford to give children so much in the way of free clinics	7	8	5	20
	115. Why schools do not give more information that will help children to make a better living (that is, higher wages)	2	1	5	8
	116. Why parents are always being asked to contribute to various school enterprises when schools are supposed to be free	2	4	2	8
	118. Why schools do not teach children to use leisure time in a more constructive way. (Criticism of children's attitude toward school and holidays)	3	2	2	7
Total number of problems—8	Number of times problems were raised by families on each income level	67	79	80	226
6.3% of the 126 problems	Per cent of number of times problems were raised by 25 families on each income level	29.6	35.3	5.3	100
	Average number of problems raised by 25 families on each income level	2.6	3.1	3.3	3.0

TABLE 25

NUMBER OF PROBLEMS ON CHILDREN AND EDUCATION BY INCOME LEVELS AND OCCUPATIONAL GROUPS

Distribution of Occupations on Various Income Levels	*Number of Families in Each Occupational Group*		*Number of Times Problems Were Raised by Each Occupational Group*		*Average Number of Problems Raised per Family in Each Occupational Group**	
$900–$1,600						
Professional	5		14		2.8	
Commercial	7		17		2.4	
Industrial	13		36		2.7	
Total		25		67		2.6
$1,600–$2,300						
Professional	7		18		2.4	
Commercial	8		26		3.2	
Industrial	10		32		3.2	
Total		25		76		3.0
$2,300–$3,000						
Professional	8		20		2.5	
Commercial	10		37		3.7	
Industrial	7		26		3.7	
Total		25		83		3.3
Total of the income ranges						
Professional	20		52		2.6	
Commercial	25		80		3.2	
Industrial	30		94		3.1	
Total		75		226		3.0

* Column 3 is obtained by dividing column 2 by column 1.

might give more information to children regarding vocational possibilities and that parents should not be taxed for various school enterprises which are supposed to be paid for by the school system, and with the wish that schools might do more to help the children form better attitudes toward the use of leisure. While problem 118, the use of leisure time, is omitted by one or more of the occupational groups in each of the income levels, the interviewer feels that many more of the parents than the table indicates had this problem on their minds and implied it in some of the other problems under health and recreation.

Table 27 shows that there are 8 problems on the topic of children and education raised 226 times by 72 families. Three of the 75

TABLE 26

DISTRIBUTION OF THE 8 PROBLEMS ON CHILDREN AND EDUCATION AMONG THE INCOME LEVELS AND OCCUPATIONAL GROUPS

Distribution of Occupations on Various Income Levels	*Total Number of Families*	*Total Number of Problems Raised by the Group*	*Numbers of the Problems Not Raised (See Table 24)*
$900–$1,600			
Professional	5	8	--
Commercial	7	5	115, 116, 118
Industrial	13	8	--
$1,600–$2,300			
Professional	7	6	116, 118
Commercial	8	6	115, 116
Industrial	10	6	115, 118
$2,300–$3,000			
Professional	8	6	94, 118
Commercial	10	8	--
Industrial	7	7	118

families raised none of these problems. Of these 3 families the principal wage-earners were a musician, a private school teacher, and an electrician. Since they raised problems on all other topics it was probably not lack of interest that caused them to omit this topic. The table shows that the largest families raise the most problems on this topic. There are more problems raised as the income increases but the gain is not as marked as the gain that occurs with the increase in the size of the family.

SUMMARY

1. There are 8 problems among the 126 which definitely relate to the topic of children and education. Among problems listed under other topics there are some which relate to this topic.

2. The number of problems is about the same on all income levels.

3. The number of problems is about the same regardless of the occupation.

4. The number of problems increases with the size of the family.

5. The 75 families raise an average of 3 problems per family regardless of income, occupation, or size.

Three families of the 75 did not raise problems on this topic.

TABLE 27

NUMBER OF PROBLEMS ON CHILDREN AND EDUCATION RAISED BY FAMILIES OF DIFFERENT SIZES AND INCOME LEVELS

Income Range and Number of Children in the Family	*Number of Families*		*Number of Problems Raised by the Families*		*Average Number of Problems per Family**	
$900–$1,200						
2 children	2		3		1.5	
3 children	1		2		2.0	
4 children	--		--		--	
Total		3		5		1.6
$1,200–$1,500						
2 children	9		22		2.4	
3 children	6		15		2.5	
4 children	--		--		--	
Total		15		37		2.4
$1,500–$1,800						
2 children	6		15		2.5	
3 children	5		17		3.4	
4 children	2		12		6.0	
Total		13		44		3.3
$1,800–$2,100						
2 children	6		14		2.3	
3 children	4		15		3.7	
4 children	1		6		6.0	
Total		11		35		3.1
$2,100–$2,400						
2 children	5		13		2.6	
3 children	2		5		2.5	
4 children	1		4		4.0	
Total		8		22		2.7
$2,400–$2,700						
2 children	5		13		2.6	
3 children	4		17		4.2	
4 children	2		10		5.0	
Total		11		40		3.6
$2,700–$3,000						
2 children	10		28		2.8	
3 children	3		11		3.3	
4 children	1		4		4.0	
Total		14		43		3.3
Total—$900–$3,000						
2 children	43		108		2.5	
3 children	25		82		3.2	
4 children	7		36		5.1	
Total		75		226		3.1

* Column 3 is obtained by dividing column 2 by column 1.

CHAPTER IX

PROBLEMS ON INSURANCE AND INVESTMENTS

The 9 problems relating to the topic of insurance and investments emerging from the interviews with the 75 families are discussed in this chapter according to the average number of problems raised by the three occupational groups and income levels and then by the number of problems raised by families of different sizes.

Problem 38 in Table 6, Chapter III, might also be listed under this topic as it relates to the question of whether one is ever justified in borrowing on one's insurance policy for other than necessities. The majority of the jury placed it under topic 9—general problems in household buying.

Table 28 lists the 9 problems relating to the topic of insurance and investments. These 9 problems occur 283 times among the 75 families, or on an average of 3.7 problems per family. The 25 families on each of the three income levels average about the same number of problems, showing about the same amount of interest in this topic on all income levels.

Table 29 shows that families within the various occupational groups average the same number of problems on each income level. Among the three occupational groups the professional group average more problems per family than either the commercial or the industrial group. However, all three groups remain close to the average of 3.7 problems raised per family regardless of occupation or income, since the professional group average 4.5 problems, the commercial group 3.7 problems, and the industrial groups 3.2 problems.

Table 30 shows that problems 101 and 113, which relate to old age pensions and the advisability of living in what seems to be an undesirable neighborhood in order to maintain an insurance policy, are the only two problems not raised by one or more families within an occupational group. Problem 101, dealing with old age pensions, does not seem to be of much interest to the families in the professional group since it is not raised by any of these families on

TABLE 28

PROBLEMS ON INSURANCE AND INVESTMENTS EMERGING FROM INTERVIEWS WITH THE 75 FAMILIES

Men and Women with Incomes from $900 to $3,000 Wanted to Know:		*Number of Families on Each Income Level Raising the Problem*			*Total Number of Families Raising the Problem*
		$900 to $1,600	*$1,600 to $2,300*	*$2,300 to $3,000*	
15. What is the basis for determining premiums for insurance		14	19	18	51
16. How much insurance should one carry on a given income		17	16	18	51
20. More about European forms of social insurance		19	16	15	50
33. What type or types of insurance are the best investment for one with a limited income		10	16	18	44
84. What is the distinction between old age insurance and old age pension		5	9	8	22
96. Arguments why women should carry insurance		8	7	4	19
97. What are the distinctions between speculation, gambling, and investments		4	8	7	19
101. Whether an adequate old age pension system would not be a good investment of public funds		6	4	7	17
113. If one should live in what seems an undesirable neighborhood in order to maintain an insurance policy		4	3	3	10
Total number of problems—9	Number of times problems were raised by families on each income level	87	98	98	283
7.1% of the 126 problems	Per cent of number of times problems were raised by 25 families on each income level	30.7	34.6	34.6	100
	Average number of problems raised by 25 families on each income level	3.4	3.9	3.9	3.7

the two lower income levels, while it does occur among the families of the commercial and industrial groups. None of the families in the industrial group raise problem 113, dealing with the question of maintaining an insurance policy at the expense of living conditions.

Table 31 shows that the 9 problems relating to the topic of in-

TABLE 29

NUMBER OF PROBLEMS ON INSURANCE AND INVESTMENTS BY INCOME LEVELS AND OCCUPATIONAL GROUPS

Distribution of Occupations on Various Income Levels	*Number of Families in Each Occupational Group*	*Number of Times Problems Were Raised by Each Occupational Group*	*Average Number of Problems Raised per Family in Each Occupational Group**
$900–$1,600			
Professional	5	20	4.0
Commercial	7	29	4.2
Industrial	13	38	2.9
Total	25	87	3.4
$1,600–$2,300			
Professional	7	32	4.5
Commercial	8	31	3.8
Industrial	10	35	3.5
Total	25	98	3.9
$2,300–$3,000			
Professional	8	39	4.3
Commercial	10	34	3.4
Industrial	7	25	3.5
Total	25	98	3.9
Total of the income ranges			
Professional	20	91	4.5
Commercial	25	94	3.7
Industrial	30	98	3.2
Total	75	283	3.7

* Column 3 is obtained by dividing column 2 by column 1.

surance and investments were raised 283 times by the 75 families, making an average of 3.7 problems per family. The income distribution apparently does not make any difference in the interest in this topic. There is a slight increase in the number of problems raised on the $2,70c–$3,000 level but that may be due to chance.

Table 31 shows that while there is no great difference in the number of problems raised on the different income levels, there is a distinction when one considers the size of the family. Families with fewer children raise more problems, as it is natural to expect since they will have more money per capita. However, in the income level $2,700–$3,000 there is one family whose principal wage-earner, a writer, raises 6 problems. Because of his education and training he

TABLE 30

DISTRIBUTION OF THE 9 PROBLEMS ON INSURANCE AND INVESTMENTS AMONG THE INCOME LEVELS AND OCCUPATIONAL GROUPS

Distribution of Occupations on Various Income Levels	*Total Number of Families*	*Total Number of Problems Raised by the Group*	*Numbers of the Problems Not Raised (See Table 28)*
$900–$1,600			
Professional	5	8	101
Commercial	7	9	--
Industrial	13	8	113
$1,600–$2,300			
Professional	7	8	101
Commercial	8	8	113
Industrial	10	8	113
$2,300–$3,000			
Professional	8	9	--
Commercial	10	8	113
Industrial	7	7	101, 113

shows an interest in a wide range of problems. Since this is an isolated case it is not fair to draw the conclusion that in the higher income levels the number of problems increases with the size of the family.

SUMMARY

1. The 9 problems on the topic of insurance and investments occur 283 times among the 75 families, making an average of 3.7 problems for each of the families regardless of income, occupation, or size of the family.

2. Among the occupational groups the professional families average 4.5 problems per family, while the commercial and industrial families average 3.7 and 3.2 problems, respectively, on the income range $900–$3,000.

3. The size of the family does not make any marked difference in the number of problems.

4. Each of the 75 families raised one or more problems on this topic.

5. Of the 9 problems, there are 7 which are raised by one or more families in each of the income levels and occupational groups.

TABLE 31

NUMBER OF PROBLEMS ON INSURANCE AND INVESTMENTS RAISED BY FAMILIES OF DIFFERENT SIZES AND INCOME LEVELS

Income Range and Number of Children in the Family	*Number of Families*		*Number of Problems Raised by the Families*		*Average Number of Problems per Family**	
$900–$1,200						
2 children	2		8		4.0	
3 children	1		2		2.0	
4 children	--		--		--	
Total		3		10		3.3
$1,200–$1,500						
2 children	9		32		3.5	
3 children	6		15		2.5	
4 children	--		--		--	
Total		15		47		3.1
$1,500–$1,800						
2 children	6		31		5.2	
3 children	5		17		3.4	
4 children	2		7		3.5	
Total		13		55		4.2
$1,800–$2,100						
2 children	6		26		4.3	
3 children	4		11		2.7	
4 children	1		3		3.0	
Total		11		40		3.6
$2,100–$2,400						
2 children	5		19		3.8	
3 children	2		10		5.0	
4 children	1		4		4.0	
Total		8		33		4.1
$2,400–$2,700						
2 children	5		18		3.6	
3 children	4		13		3.2	
4 children	2		5		2.5	
Total		11		36		3.2
$2,700–$3,000						
2 children	10		42		4.2	
3 children	3		14		4.6	
4 children	1		6		6.0	
Total		14		62		4.4
Total—$900–$3,000						
2 children	43		176		4.0	
3 children	25		82		3.2	
4 children	7		25		3.5	
Total		75		283		3.7

* Column 3 is obtained by dividing column 2 by column 1.

CHAPTER X

PROBLEMS ON WAGES AND EMPLOYMENT

The 5 problems relating to the topic of wages and employment are discussed in this chapter according to the number of problems raised by the 25 families on each of the three income levels, the number of problems raised by the various occupational groups, and then by the number of problems raised by families of different sizes.

Table 32 gives the list of 5 problems on wages and employment emerging from the interviews. These are numbered the same as in Table 6, Chapter III, page 14, so that one gets some idea of their relative position in that list of 126 problems. These 5 problems occurred 166 times during the interviews with the 75 families, making an average of 2.2 problems for each family. The 25 families on the the lowest income level, $900–$1,600, raised them 51 times, or 30 per cent of the total number of times they occur. The 25 families on the two higher income levels raised them 55 and 60 times each, or 33 and 36 per cent, respectively, of the occurrences. This would indicate that as the income increases there is an increase in the interest shown in these problems of wages and employment, since more families raise them during the interviews.

Table 33 gives the average number of problems on wages and employment by income levels and occupational groups and then a total for the occupational groups regardless of the income. We find that among the 25 families on the income level ranging from $900 to $1,600 there are 5 whose principal wage-earners are engaged in the professional occupations. These families raised problems on wages and employment 8 times, making an average of 1.6 problems for each family. The commercial and industrial groups average 2.1 problems for each family. The average of the 25 families is 2 problems. The average number of problems on wages and employment for families in each occupation on the various income levels shows little increase as the income increases.

The 20 families in the professional group average 3.1 problems for each family on the income range of $900-$3,000. This exceeds

TABLE 32

PROBLEMS ON WAGES AND EMPLOYMENT EMERGING FROM THE INTERVIEWS WITH THE 75 FAMILIES

Men and Women with Incomes from $900 to $3,000 Wanted to Know:		*Number of Families on Each Income Level Raising the Problem*			*Total Number of Families Raising the Problem*
		$900 to $1,600	*$1,600 to $2,300*	*$2,300 to $3,000*	
6. What constructive work is being done to equalize wages and cost of living; if employers should not feel greater responsibility for increasing wages when living costs increase		18	20	19	57
45. Why public employment bureaus are so inadequate		14	10	13	37
57. What justification there is for the lower wages of women		12	9	11	32
91. How can one plan to buy systematically if income is uncertain; if there should not be unemployment insurance to prevent haphazard buying		5	9	7	21
95. If overspecialization is not one of the great difficulties in the way of a skilled laborer's finding employment in the present business depression		2	7	10	19
Total number of problems—5	Number of times families on each income level raised these problems	51	55	60	166
3.9% of the 126 problems	Per cent of number of times problems were raised by 25 families on each income level	30.7	33.1	36.1	100
	Average number of problems raised by 25 families on each income level	2.0	2.2	2.4	2.2

the averages for the commercial and industrial groups, which are 1.9 and 2.4 problems, respectively. The fact that the commercial group does not raise as many problems as the professional and industrial groups may be due to the number of civil service employees in it whose salaries are not affected by changing business conditions.

Table 34 shows that problem 45, which relates to the inadequacy of public employment bureaus, was not raised by the professional group of families on either of the two lower income levels. This

TABLE 33

NUMBER OF PROBLEMS ON WAGES AND EMPLOYMENT BY INCOME LEVELS AND OCCUPATIONAL GROUPS

Distribution of Occupations on Various Income Levels	*Number of Families in Each Occupational Group*		*Number of Times Problems Were Raised by Each Occupational Group*		*Average Number of Problems Raised per Family in Each Occupational Group**	
$900–$1,600						
Professional	5		8		1.6	
Commercial	7		15		2.1	
Industrial	13		28		2.1	
Total		25		51		2.0
$1,600–$2,300						
Professional	7		14		2.0	
Commercial	8		13		1.6	
Industrial	10		28		2.8	
Total		25		55		2.2
$2,300–$3,000						
Professional	8		21		2.6	
Commercial	10		21		2.1	
Industrial	7		18		2.5	
Total		25		60		2.4
Total of the income ranges						
Professional	20		43		3.1	
Commercial	25		49		1.9	
Industrial	30		74		2.4	
Total		75		166		2.2

* Column 3 is obtained by dividing column 2 by column 1.

may be explained by the fact that the public employment bureaus usually have more positions open for commercial and industrial workers and therefore the professional group of workers is not as likely to patronize them. This problem occurs among the commercial and industrial groups on all three income levels. Problem 91 is of more or less theoretical interest to all groups rather than of interest to any one group, since it deals with the possibility of systematic buying when income is uncertain.

Table 35 shows the number of problems on wages and employment raised by families of different sizes and income levels. There are 5 families who do not raise any problems relating to this topic. These wage-earners are 4 patrolmen and a Hebrew teacher. The

TABLE 34

DISTRIBUTION OF THE 12 PROBLEMS ON WAGES AND EMPLOYMENT AMONG THE INCOME LEVELS AND OCCUPATIONAL GROUPS

Distribution of Occupations on Various Income Levels	*Total Number of Families*	*Total Number of Problems Raised by the Group*	*Numbers of the Problems Not Raised (See Table 16)*
$900–$1,600			
Professional	5	4	45
Commercial	7	5	--
Industrial	13	4	91
$1,600–$2,300			
Professional	7	4	45
Commercial	8	4	91
Industrial	10	5	--
$2,300–$3,000			
Professional	8	5	--
Commercial	10	5	--
Industrial	7	5	--

70 families who raise problems relating to this topic bring them up 166 times, making an average of 2.3 problems for all families irrespective of size of family or income. The summary for the table shows that apparently the size of the family does not make any difference in the number of problems raised. As the income increases there is a tendency for more problems to occur.

SUMMARY

1. The 5 problems on the topic relating to wages and employment occur 166 times among the 70 families, an average of 2.2 problems for each of the families regardless of its income, occupation, or size.

2. Occupational distribution does not seem to make any marked distinction in the number of problems raised relating to wages and employment. Professional families tend to raise more problems, but in general all occupational groups show the same interest.

3. There is no marked increase in the number of problems as the income increases.

4. The size of the family does not seem to make any marked difference in the number or type of problems raised.

5. Five families did not raise any problems on this topic.

TABLE 35

NUMBER OF PROBLEMS ON WAGES AND EMPLOYMENT RAISED BY FAMILIES OF DIFFERENT SIZES AND INCOME LEVELS

Income Range and Number of Children in the Family	*Number of Families*	*Number of Problems Raised by the Families*	*Average Number of Problems per Family***
$900–$1,200			
2 children	2	3	1.5
3 children	1	1	1.0
4 children	--	--	--
Total	3	4	1.3
$1,200–$1,500			
2 children	9	19	2.1
3 children	6	15	2.5
4 children	--	--	--
Total	15	34	2.2
$1,500–$1,800			
2 children	6	15	2.5
3 children	5*	10	2.0
4 children	2	3	1.5
Total	13	28	2.1
$1,800–$2,100			
2 children	6	13	2.1
3 children	4*	5	1.6
4 children	1	2	2.0
Total	11	20	1.8
$2,100–$2,400			
2 children	5*	10	2.5
3 children	2	8	4.0
4 children	1	2	2.0
Total	8	20	2.8
$2,400–$2,700			
2 children	5*	12	3.0
3 children	4	9	3.0
4 children	2*	1	1.0
Total	11	22	2.0
$2,700–$3,000			
2 children	10	29	2.9
3 children	3	8	2.6
4 children	1	1	1.0
Total	14	38	2.7
Total—$900–$3,000			
2 children	43	101	2.3
3 children	25	56	2.0
4 children	7	9	1.2
Total	75	166	2.2

* 1 family not reporting.

** Column 3 is obtained by dividing column 2 by column 1.

CHAPTER XI

PROBLEMS OF GENERAL ECONOMIC INTEREST

There are 30 problems of general economic interest. Several might be placed under topic 9, general problems in household buying. Table 36 shows the list of 30 problems relating to general economic problems as taken from the list of 126 in Chapter III. The same numbering is used as in that chapter so that one may get some idea of their relative position in the whole group of 126 problems.

The 25 families on the lowest income level, \$900–\$1,600, raised the problems about 28 per cent of the 693 times that they are mentioned. The per cents increase to 33 and 39 as the income increases to the \$1,600–\$2,300 and \$2,300–\$3,000 levels. This would indicate that as their incomes increase the families show more interest in general economic problems.

Table 37 indicates the frequency with which the 30 problems on general economics were raised by the three occupational groups within the three income levels, and then the frequency with which each occupational group raised the problems without regard to the income. Among the 75 families interviewed, 25 fall into the income group ranging from \$900 to \$1,600. Among these 25 are 5 whose principal wage-earners are engaged in the professional occupations. These families average 8.6 problems. The families in the commercial group average 9.2, and in the industrial group 6.6. The average for the 25 families is 7.7 problems regardless of occupation.

The average for the 25 families on each income level increases with the increase in income. On the highest income level the industrial families average 13 problems per family, which is more than the averages of either of the other two groups on this income level. This is probably due to the fact that these industrial workers are all union men and the increase in the number of problems is due to a combination of the educational work of the unions and the increased income which makes for an increased leisure.

The 75 families, regardless of income or occupation, raised these

TABLE 36

PROBLEMS OF GENERAL ECONOMIC INTEREST EMERGING FROM THE INTERVIEWS WITH THE 75 FAMILIES

Men and Women with Incomes from $900 to $3,000 Wanted to Know:	*Number of Families on Each Income Level Raising the Problem*			*Total Number of Families Raising the Problem*
	$900 to $1,600	*$1,600 to $2,300*	*$2,300 to $3,000*	
3. What is causing the present business depression	19	20	21	60
10. Why the rich should not be taxed more heavily to secure more nearly equal distribution of incomes and opportunity	20	19	15	54
14. Why poverty must exist; why there is not a more nearly equal distribution of money	17	15	19	51
19. Why the United States is called such a prosperous country when there is so much poverty and unemployment	17	15	19	51
34. Whether one can tell definitely how much machinery is causing unemployment by displacing men	15	14	14	43
35. How present inheritance laws could be changed to produce a more nearly equal distribution of money	18	14	10	42
39. Why certain stores can offer cut rates, and the effect on other stores	10	15	15	40
59. How a tariff affects food prices	8	7	16	21
69. What is a woman's time in the home worth	7	8	12	27
70. What general connection exists between the terms—tariff, monopoly, public utilities—and the individual household	7	8	12	27
72. More about the relationship of price and quality	8	10	9	27
85. What is the effect on food prices of paying cash or of obtaining credit	4	8	10	22
87. What effect has the extensive sale of accessories on the employment situation, prices, etc.	0	10	11	21
89. What causes fluctuations in prices in general	4	8	9	21
90. Arguments for and against husbands and wives sharing equally in household expenses (On the wife's working part or full time)	4	6	11	21
92. What is meant by public revenues; how they are obtained, and the relation they bear to free parks, etc.	9	5	7	21

TABLE 36 (*Continued*)

Men and Women with Incomes from $900 to $3,000 Wanted to Know:	*Number of Families on Each Income Level Raising the Problem*			*Total Number of Families Raising the Problem*
	$900 to $1,600	*$1,600 to $2,300*	*$2,300 to $3,000*	
93. More about the organization of the Stock Exchange	1	8	12	21
100. What is meant by household capital goods	7	6	4	17
103. Whether the efficient functioning of the Farm Board will result in a radical lowering of food costs	2	6	7	15
106. What justification stores have for charging more in certain sections of the city even though rents may be similar in the various sections	2	7	5	14
109. How mass production and standardization of articles, such as felt hats, affects the price	0	6	7	13
110. What is meant by the purchasing power of the dollar. What is meant by the changing value of the dollar	2	3	8	13
112. If there would be any radical lowering if prices of women's clothes were as standardized as men's are	2	5	4	11
117. What effect the present restriction of immigration will have on the labor market eventually	2	4	2	8
119. More about the economic relation between a shorter working week and increased leisure; and if the increased leisure would not cost the working man more, because of greater opportunity to acquire more expensive habits	1	2	3	6
122. How far competition regulates prices and wages; how far monopolistic control regulates them	2	1	1	4
123. How can the capitalist class justify the statement that the United States offers equal opportunities	2	1	1	4
124. If there is any possibility that milk will, like gas, be declared a public utility	2	1	0	3
125. Whether consumers' clubs as advocated by Chase and Schlink will ever be developed in a practical way	2	1	0	3
126. What is meant by the saying that the prosperity of the country depends upon the inequality of income, since this makes for greater capital accumulation	2	0	0	2

TABLE 36 (*Continued*)

Men and Women with Incomes from $900 to $3,000 Wanted to Know:		*Number of Families on Each Income Level Raising the Problem* $900 to $1,600	$1,600 to $2,300	$2,300 to $3,000	*Total Number of Families Raising the Problem*
Total number of problems—30	Number of times families on each income level raised these problems	194	231	268	693
23.8% of the 126 problems	Per cent of number of times problems were raised by 25 families on each income level	27.9%	33.3%	38.6%	100%
	Average number of problems raised by 25 families on each income level	7.7	9.2	10.7	9.2

30 problems 693 times, making an average of 9.2 problems for each family. When the 75 families are separated into the three occupational groups without regard for the three income levels, one finds that the occupational groups remain close to the average of 9.2 problems for the 75 families. This would indicate that occupational distribution does not make for any marked distinction in their interest in general economic problems.

Table 38 shows the distribution of the problems among the families of various occupations on the three income levels. The table does not indicate the frequency with which these problems were raised. In order to find the frequency with which the problems were raised, this table can be read as follows in connection with the preceding table. For example, the 5 professional families on the lowest income level, $900–$1,600, raised 19 problems 43 times, making an average of 8.6 problems for each family. The last column of this table shows the numbers of the problems which these various occupational groups omitted. One finds many problems in this list of problems which were omitted by the different groups. This would indicate that the interest of the various occupational groups is not centered in a few economic problems but in many and that the same problems do not interest all groups. Since there are many problems listed in this column, it is easier

TABLE 37

NUMBER OF PROBLEMS OF GENERAL ECONOMIC INTEREST BY INCOME LEVELS AND OCCUPATIONAL GROUPS

Distribution of Occupations on Various Income Levels	*Number of Families in Each Occupational Group*		*Number of Times Problems Were Raised by Each Occupational Group*		*Average Number of Problems Raised per Family in Each Occupational Group**	
$900–$1,600						
Professional	5		43		8.6	
Commercial	7		65		9.2	
Industrial	13		86		6.6	
Total		25		194		7.7
$1,600–$2,300						
Professional	7		70		10.0	
Commercial	8		71		8.8	
Industrial	10		90		9.0	
Total		25		231		9.2
$2,300–$3,000						
Professional	8		88		11.0	
Commercial	10		86		8.6	
Industrial	7		94		13.3	
Total		25		268		10.7
Total of the income ranges						
Professional	20		201		10.0	
Commercial	25		222		8.8	
Industrial	30		270		9.0	
Total		75		693		9.2

* Column 3 is obtained by dividing column 2 by column 1.

to enumerate the problems common to all groups. We find that problems 3, 10, 14, 19, 34, 35, 39, 59, 69, 70, 72, 85, 89 are raised by one or more families in each occupational group on the various income levels. These problems are all closely related to those of wages and employment and include several on taxation, inheritance, and relationship between price and quality.

Table 38 shows also that there are 16 problems in which there is a scattering of interest, leaving 14 problems which are raised by each occupational group regardless of income.

Table 39 shows that each of the 75 families raised one or more of the problems relating to general economics. Since the 30 problems were raised by the 75 families 693 times, there is an average

TABLE 38

DISTRIBUTION OF THE 30 PROBLEMS OF GENERAL ECONOMIC INTEREST AMONG THE INCOME LEVELS AND OCCUPATIONAL GROUPS

Distribution of Occupations on Various Income Levels	*Total Number of Families*	*Total Number of Problems Raised by the Group*	*Numbers of the Problems Not Raised (See Table 36)*
$900–$1,600			
Professional	5	19	87, 92, 100, 106, 109, 112, 117, 123, 122, 124, 126
Commercial	7	20	87, 93, 106, 109, 110, 119, 123, 124, 125, 126
Industrial	13	16	69, 70, 85, 87, 89, 103, 109, 110, 93, 117, 119, 122, 124, 125
$1,600–$2,300			
Professional	7	23	89, 92, 102, 117, 123, 124, 126
Commercial	8	22	92, 100, 119, 123, 124, 125, 126, 122
Industrial	10	22	69, 90, 103, 110, 119, 125, 122, 126
$2,300–$3,000			
Professional	8	22	108, 109, 119, 122, 123, 124, 125, 126
Commercial	10	24	100, 117, 123, 124, 125, 126
Industrial	7	24	103, 106, 117, 122, 125, 126

of 9.2 problems for each family, regardless of size, income, or occupation. One finds that the 43 families with 2 children average 9.2 problems for each family on the income range of $900–$1,600. Families with 3 and 4 children raise 9 and 8.5 problems, respectively, which indicates that the size of the family does not determine the number of problems or the interest in these problems. There is no great distinction between the average number of problems raised by families of different sizes on the different incomes. In the income range of $2,700–$3,000 there is one family with 4 children where the principal wage-earner is a writer. As on several of the other topics this family raised many more problems than any other family.

In general one may say that the size of the family does not determine the interest in economic problems. As is true with so

TABLE 39

NUMBER OF PROBLEMS OF GENERAL ECONOMIC INTEREST RAISED BY FAMILIES OF DIFFERENT SIZES AND INCOME LEVELS

Income Range and Number of Children in the Family	*Number of Families*	*Number of Problems Raised by the Families*	*Average Number of Problems per Family**
$900–$1,200			
2 children	2	17	8.5
3 children	1	6	6.0
4 children	--	--	--
Total	3	23	7.6
$1,200–$1,500			
2 children	9	69	7.8
3 children	6	48	8.0
4 children	--	--	--
Total	15	117	7.8
$1,500–$1,800			
2 children	6	69	11.5
3 children	5	39	7.8
4 children	2	8	4.0
Total	13	116	8.9
$1,800–$2,100			
2 children	6	52	8.6
3 children	4	30	7.5
4 children	1	7	7.0
Total	11	89	8.0
$2,100–$2,400			
2 children	5	47	9.4
3 children	2	25	12.5
4 children	1	8	8.0
Total	8	80	10.0
$2,400–$2,700			
2 children	5	62	12.4
3 children	4	44	11.0
4 children	2	21	10.5
Total	11	127	11.5
$2,700–$3,000			
2 children	10	92	9.2
3 children	3	33	11.0
4 children	1	16	16.0
Total	14	141	10.7
Total—$900–$3,000			
2 children	43	408	9.2
3 children	25	225	9.0
4 children	7	60	8.5
Total	75	693	9.2

* Column 3 is obtained by dividing column 2 by column 1.

many of the topics, one finds that as the income increases there are more families raising problems.

Summary

1. The 30 problems on the topic relating to general economics occur 693 times among the 75 families, making an average of 9.2 problems for each family regardless of income, occupation, or size of the family.
2. Each of the 75 families raised one or more problems on this topic.
3. As the income increases there is an increase in the average number of problems per family regardless of occupational distribution.
4. Families in the various occupational groups average about the same number of problems regardless of income.
5. Families of various sizes average about the same number of problems.
6. There are 14 of the 30 problems which are raised by families of each occupational group on each income level. No one group shows special interest in any particular problem or problems.

CHAPTER XII

PROBLEMS OF GENERAL INTEREST TO THE HOUSEHOLD

There are 13 problems which relate so closely to the topics of food, clothing, and housing that they might be listed under each of these topics. It seemed best to make a seperate list of these problems and in Chapters IV, V, and VI mention that these problems are so closely related that they should be included with them. The same numbering is used for the problems in Table 40 as in Table 6, page 14, in order to give some idea of their relative position in that list of 126 problems.

The 75 families raised these 13 problems 460 times. The 25 families on the lowest income level raised them 120 times, or 26 per cent of the total number of times. On the middle income level, $1,600–$2,300, the problems occur 167 times, or 36 per cent of the total number of times, while the 25 families on the $2,300–$3,000 income level raised them 173 times, or 37 per cent of the total number of times. This shows that as the income increases there seems to be an increase in the interest shown in these problems since more families bring them up in the interviews. The difference, however, is only about 1 per cent between the two higher income levels and there is only a 10 per cent difference in the total income range.

Table 41 gives the total number of times the problems have been raised by income levels. This table also shows the frequency with which these problems are raised by occupational groups within the income levels. Among the 25 families on the lowest income level these problems occur 120 times, making an average of 6.1 problems for each family. The group of professional families within this income level raises the problems on an average of 6 problems per family. The commercial and industrial groups average 4 problems each.

On the next income level the 25 families average slightly more than 6 problems for each family, with the professional and com-

TABLE 40

PROBLEMS ON GENERAL HOUSEHOLD BUYING EMERGING FROM PERSONAL INTERVIEWS WITH 75 FAMILIES

Men and Women with Incomes from $900 to $3,000 Wanted to Know:		*Number of Families on Each Income Level Raising the Problem*			*Total Number of Families Raising the Problem*
		$900 to $1,600	*$1,600 to $2,300*	*$2,300 to $3,000*	
5. Why food prices fluctuate so much more than prices of other household commodities		19	20	20	59
27. How to take advantage of sales and if there is a saving in money in the initial cost at the expense of quality		19	17	10	46
29. More about the economics of installment buying		17	12	16	45
36. The significance of the different types of markets		10	22	9	41
38. If one is justified in borrowing on one's insurance policy for other than necessities		12	14	14	40
43. Why labels do not tell the consumer what she needs to know (use,quality,amount,etc.)		10	14	14	38
49. Where to obtain information about weights and measures		7	12	16	35
52. How much a brand name insures a standardized quality of goods		2	16	15	33
61. How much actual saving there is in the home preparation of food; for example, bread		8	12	11	31
65. Whether it would not lower prices to buy direct from the producer		0	12	18	30
73. If it is possible for the consumer to get better style and quality at lower prices		7	6	14	27
78. Whether trading at one satisfactory store would tend to eliminate competition and affect food prices		2	8	16	26
114. If employment conditions could not be shown on the label so the consumer might have a chance to buy only goods made under the best conditions		7	2	0	9
Total number of problems—13	Number of times families on each income level raised these problems	120	167	173	460
10.3% of the 126 problems	Per cent of number of times problems were raised by 25 families on each income level	26	36.3	37.6	100
	Average number of problems raised by 25 families on each income level	4.8	6.6	6.9	6.1

TABLE 41

NUMBER OF PROBLEMS OF GENERAL INTEREST TO HOUSEHOLD BUYING BY INCOME LEVELS AND OCCUPATIONAL GROUPS

Distribution of Occupations on Various Income Levels	*Number of Families in Each Occupational Group*	*Number of Times Problems Were Raised by Each Occupational Group*	*Average Number of Problems Raised per Family in Each Occupational Group**
$900–$1,600			
Professional	5	30	6.0
Commercial	7	34	4.8
Industrial	13	56	4.3
Total	25	120	4.8
$1,600–$2,300			
Professional	7	51	7.2
Commercial	8	56	7.0
Industrial	10	60	6.0
Total	25	167	6.6
$2,300–$3,000			
Professional	8	61	7.6
Commercial	10	69	6.9
Industrial	7	43	6.1
Total	25	173	6.9
Total of the income ranges			
Professional	20	142	7.1
Commercial	25	159	6.3
Industrial	30	159	5.3
Total	75	460	6.1

* Column 3 is obtained by dividing column 2 by column 1.

mercial groups averaging 7 problems each and the industrial group 6 problems. This is an increase in the average number of problems per family.

On the highest income level the average remains about the same as on the middle income level, with the professional families averaging slightly more than the other two occupational groups. When the three income levels are averaged together, one finds that the professional families average 7 problems for each of the 20 families in this group while the 25 commercial and 30 industrial families average 6 and 5 problems each. Since the average for the 75 families, regardless of occupation or income, was 6.1 problems for each family, one finds that the professional families raise slightly

TABLE 42

DISTRIBUTION OF THE 13 PROBLEMS OF GENERAL INTEREST TO HOUSEHOLD BUYING AMONG THE INCOME LEVELS AND OCCUPATIONAL GROUPS

Distribution of Occupations on Various Income Levels	*Total Number of Families*	*Total Number of Problems Raised by the Group*	*Numbers of the Problems Not Raised (See Table 40)*
$900–$1,600			
Professional	5	11	65, 114
Commercial	7	12	65
Industrial	13	10	52, 65, 78
$1,600–$2,300			
Professional	7	12	114
Commercial	8	12	114
Industrial	10	12	73
$2,300–$3,000			
Professional	8	12	114
Commercial	10	12	114
Industrial	7	11	36,114

more than the average and the industrial families raise slightly less than the average.

Table 41 gives the frequency with which the problems occur by occupational groups and income levels. Table 42 shows the distribution of the 13 problems among the same groups as shown in the previous table. For example, one finds that the 5 professional families on the $900–$1,600 income range raise 11 of the 13 problems on this topic, but omit problems 65 and 114 which relate to the possibility of saving in buying direct from the producer and of giving employment conditions on the label. Column 3 shows that problems 65 and 114 do not occur in several of the groups. The professional group of families omits only 2 of the total number of 13 problems among the three income levels. The commercial group omits the same problems, while the industrial group omits in addition problem 52, relating to the extent that the brand name insures standardized goods, problem 73, dealing with the possibility of the consumer getting better style and quality at lower prices, and problem 36, dealing with the justification of borrowing on one's insurance policy in order to buy other than absolute necessities.

TABLE 43

NUMBER OF PROBLEMS OF GENERAL HOUSEHOLD INTEREST RAISED BY FAMILIES OF DIFFERENT SIZES AND INCOME LEVELS

Income Range and Number of Children in the Family	*Number of Families*		*Number of Problems Raised by the Families*		*Average Number of Problems per Family**	
$900–$1,200						
2 children	2		8		4	
3 children	1		3		3	
4 children	--		--		--	
Total		3		11		3.3
$1,200–$1,500						
2 children	9		41		4.5	
3 children	6		31		5.1	
4 children	--		--		--	
Total		15		72		4.1
$1,500–$1,800						
2 children	6		43		7.1	
3 children	5		26		5.2	
4 children	2		12		6.0	
Total		13		81		6.2
$1,800–$2,100						
2 children	6		35		5.8	
3 children	4		28		7.0	
4 children	1		3		3.0	
Total		11		66		6.0
$2,100–$2,400						
2 children	5		32		6.4	
3 children	2		16		8.0	
4 children	1		9		9.0	
Total		8		57		7.1
$2,400–$2,700						
2 children	5		34		6.8	
3 children	4		26		6.5	
4 children	2		12		6.0	
Total		11		72		6.5
$2,700–$3,000						
2 children	10		69		6.9	
3 children	3		22		7.3	
4 children	1		10		10.0	
Total		14		101		7.2
Total—$900–$3,000						
2 children	43		262		6.0	
3 children	25		152		6.0	
4 children	7		46		6.5	
Total		75		460		6.1

* Column 3 is obtained by dividing column 2 by column 1.

Table 43 shows the number of problems on household buying raised by families of different sizes and income levels. Among the total of 75 families there are 43 families with two children each. These 43 families raise the 13 problems on this topic 262 times, making an average of 6 problems for each of the families. The 25 families with 3 children each and the 7 families with 4 children each average 6 problems; or so very little more that one cannot conclude that the size of the family determines the interest in these problems. The table shows that as the income increases families tend to raise more problems, since on the lowest income range, $900–$1,200, the 3 families average only 3 problems per family while on the highest income range, $2,700–$3,000, the 14 families average 7 problems.

Summary

1. The 13 problems on the topic relating to general problems in household buying emerge 460 times among the 75 families, making an average of 6 problems per family regardless of income, occupation, or size of the family.

2. As the income increases there is an increase in the average number of problems raised by families on the $900–$1,600 level to the $1,600–$2,300 level, while the average remains the same between the middle and highest income levels.

3. The professional families average 7 problems for each family regardless of income, while the commercial and industrial families average 6 and 5 problems each.

4. The size of the family does not make any difference in the number of problems raised by the families. But families on the lower income levels average fewer problems per family.

5. The 13 problems are uniformly distributed throughout the income levels and occupational groups; that is, 10 of the 13 problems are raised by one or more families on each income level and occupational group.

6. Each one of the 75 families raised one or more problems on this topic.

CHAPTER XIII

SUMMARY OF CHAPTERS III TO XII INCLUSIVE

Observed Standards of Living

The preceding discussion of the problems has not taken into account any phase of the interview other than the actual problems raised by the families at that time. If one could take each of the 75 families as an individual case study, interesting contrasts would be found in their standards of living. For example, the interviewer found in the home of a man whose income as a garbage collector ranges from $1,900 to $2,100 an atmosphere of peace and happiness not found in many of the other places visited. The two children, a boy of 12 and a girl of 8, were both attending the public schools. The interviewer saw this home in the evening where she found the father reading aloud while his wife sewed. The wife was not very strong and was in the habit of doing some sewing and darning for a woman who paid her by cleaning the apartment once a week. The family took books regularly from the library. Since they had so many of the more expensive magazines on the table the interviewer asked if they subscribed. The man was much amused and wanted to know where they could find the money for subscriptions on their limited income. He explained that he often found clean copies of the magazines when he collected the garbage in the mornings from the uptown apartment houses. His wife clipped pictures and poems from these magazines after they had been read and was making scrapbooks to amuse the children on rainy days. Their apartment was very clean and well furnished with rather worn furniture which had apparently been given to them some years before. Even on the limited income they were managing to save a little money, carry a small life insurance, dress the children with some degree of taste, although this was at the expense of new clothing for the wife. The man wore a uniform during his working hours which lowered the clothing expenses. They had practically no recreation outside the home, but depended upon each other. They lived near enough to Central Park to walk there occasionally in the evening for the open-air concerts. The family had apparently nothing to do with the other families in the house, partly because of their natural reserve and partly because they felt rather superior to the other families who had been in this country only a short time.

MONTHLY BUDGET FOR FAMILY OF GARBAGE COLLECTOR
Income range $1,900–$2,100

Man, wife, 2 children
March, 1930

Food	$66.00	40%
Clothing	21.00	13
Rent, Fuel, Light	39.00	24
Operating Expense	14.00	8
Health, Recreation, Education	5.00	3
Savings	20.00	12
	$165.00	100%

In contrast to this home was the home of a private school teacher with an income ranging from $2,900 to $3,100. The home was not well kept, the three children were irritable and cross, and there was about the place a general atmosphere of unrest. The difference in the occupation made the clothing expenses of this family necessarily higher, particularly for the man. Both the man and his wife had attended college, although the wife did not graduate. They were living beyond their income and the wife seemed to be making no effort to reduce expenses. As far as one could judge she was trying to maintain a standard of living for an income far beyond their means. The husband had been keeping account of their expenses in an effort to show her how their finances stood. That account follows and also for comparison a budget worked out by the Metropolitan Life Insurance Company for families of the same size and income. (See page 83.)

In the cases of these two families the income had been the same for several years, so that there had been no decided change in their standards of living due to change in amount of money they had to spend. In the cases of the families of two musicians there had been a drop in income from around $3,000 to $1,000. One musician had lost his regular work through the change in type of music in the moving picture theatre in which he had been regularly

Typical Monthly Budget for Family of Teacher Income range $2,900–$3,100 March, 1930			Budget worked out by the Metropolitan Life Insurance Company for a family of man, wife and 3 children, with income of $2,900–$3,000	
Food	$80.00	32%	$75.00	30%
Clothing	55.00	22	37.50	15
Rent, Fuel, Light	70.00	28	62.50	25
Operating Expense	22.00	9	27.50	11
*Health, Education, Recreation	13.00	5	17.50	7
Savings and Insurance	10.00	4	30.00	12
	$250.00	100%	$250.00	100%

* Includes amounts given to church, etc.

employed. In the other family the husband had had a long illness and was unable to find regular employment. Both of these families received aid from various organizations for a short period but were at the time self-supporting except for help when there was illness in the family. Their homes were well kept. Any furniture which could be spared had been sold so that they had only the bare necessities. The children were in school and the parents hoped that they could remain in school until they graduated from high school. Since both of these families had received aid from various organizations they were in the habit of keeping an account of their expenses. The monthly budget for the two families is very similar.

Monthly Budget of Family of Musician
Income $1,000

Man, wife, two children
February, 1930

Food	$35.00	42%
Clothing	10.00	12
Rent, Fuel, Light	30.00	36
Operating Expenses	8.00	10
Health, Recreation, Education	.....	..
Savings	.....	..
	$83.00	100%

In the majority of the homes one found well-kept, clean apartments (or rather tenements). Few of the families had more than three rooms, only 8 lived in elevator apartment houses, and only 10 had telephones in their apartments. Not one of these 75 families had an automobile. Few had radios, although among the industrial families was found a group of four who owned a radio in common which was placed in a common living room. Most of the families depended upon the movies and free outdoor concerts for their amusements. Among the women of the professional group of families there seemed to be more card-playing than among the women in the other two groups. These women entertained more in their homes than the women of the commercial and industrial families, which made the food item in their budgets proportionately larger than that of the other two groups. Their clothing expenditures were also larger for this reason, but they made more of their own clothes for everyday use than did the women in the other groups. Practically all the families were carrying life insurance. There did not seem to be any difference between the groups in the type or amount of insurance, that is, as far as the interviewer could judge, since this seemed to be one question which they did not like to discuss except to show that they wanted to know more about it.

While the professional class spent more for food, shelter, and clothing than the other two income groups, they also managed to maintain a better standard of living so far as outward appearances revealed. All groups were equally interested in problems of investment, but the professional group were more interested in old age protection while the other groups looked for old age pension relief.

Table 44 shows that the 25 families at the income level $900–$1,600 raised 118 of the 126 problems. These problems occurred 1,002 times during the interviews. The 25 families at the middle income level raised 125 of the 126 problems. These occurred 1,354 times during the interviews. The 25 families at the highest income level, $2,300–$3,000, raised 123 of the 126 problems. These occurred 1,526 times. The 126 problems occurred a total of 3,882 times among the 75 families. The table indicates that as the income increases a greater interest is shown in these problems, since at the lowest income levels families raise an average of 40 problems apiece, while the average number of problems increases to 54 at the middle income level and to 61 at the highest income level.

Within the various topic divisions of the problems one finds that among five topics—problems on food, clothing, and housing, problems of general economic interest, and problems in the buying of household supplies—the problems occur more times as the income increases. Among the four topics dealing with health and recreation,

TABLE 44

NUMBER OF PROBLEMS ON THE 9 TOPICS RAISED BY FAMILIES ON DIFFERENT INCOME LEVELS

Topic	*Number of Problems Raised by Each Income Level*	*Total Number of Problems on Each Topic*	*Number of Times Problems Were Raised by 25 Families on Each Income Level*	*Total Number of Times Problems Were Raised by 75 Families*	*Average Number of Problems Raised by Families**
1. Food and Food Buying ..		32		1,096	
$ 900–$1,600	30		259		10.3
1,600– 2,300	32		381		15.2
2,300– 3,000	32		456		18.2
2. Clothing		12		412	
$ 900–$1,600	11		65		2.6
1,600– 2,300	12		161		6.4
2,300– 3,000	12		186		7.4
3. Housing and Equipment .		12			
$ 900–$1,600	11		113	413	4.6
1,600– 2,300	12		142		5.6
2,300– 3,000	12		158		6.3
4. Health and Recreation ..		5		133	
$ 900–$1,600	5		46		1.8
1,600– 2,300	5		43		1.3
2,300– 3,000	5		44		1.3
5. Children and Education .		8		226	
$ 900–$1,600	8		67		2.6
1,600– 2,300	8		76		3.0
2,300– 3,300	8		83		3.3
6. Insurance and Investment		9		283	
$ 900–$1,600	9		87		3.4
1,600– 2,300	9		98		3.9
2,300– 3,000	9		98		3.9
7. Wages and Employment .		5		166	
$ 900–$1,600	5		51		2.0
1,600– 2,300	5		55		2.0
2,300– 3,000	5		60		2.4

TABLE 44 (*Continued*)

Topic	*Number of Problems Raised by Each Income Level*	*Total Number of Problems on Each Topic*	*Number of Times Problems Were Raised by 25 Families on Each Income Level*	*Total Number of Times Problems Were Raised by 75 Families*	*Average Number of Problems Raised by Families**
8. General Economic Problems		30		693	
$ 900–$1,600	27		194		7.7
1,600– 2,300	28		231		9.2
2,300– 3,000	28		269		10.7
9. General Problems in Household Buying . . .		13		460	
$ 900–$1,600	12		120		4.8
1,600– 3,300	13		167		6.6
2,300– 3,000	12		173		6.9
Total Number of Problems .		126		3,882	
$ 900–$1,600	118		1,002		40.0
1,600– 2,300	125		1,354		54.1
2,300– 3,000	123		1,526		61.0

* Obtained by dividing column 3 by 25 families on each income level.

children and education, insurance and investments, and wages and employment, the problems occur so nearly the same number of times at each of the three income levels that one cannot say that the income makes any difference.

Table 47 shows that there is a slight tendency for the families with more children to raise more problems when all 126 problems are considered. When these 126 problems are discussed under the nine topic headings, one finds that families with 4 children raise more problems than do families with 2 and 3 children in only the topics dealing with housing and equipment and children and education.

In the preceding chapters the 126 problems have been discussed under the headings of the nine topic divisions. All the tables from these chapters which relate to the average number of problems raised by families in the different occupational groups are summarized in Table 46. This table shows that the professional groups

TABLE 45

NUMBER OF PROBLEMS ON THE 9 TOPICS RAISED BY FAMILIES ON DIFFERENT INCOME LEVELS AND OCCUPATIONAL GROUPS

Topic and Group	*Average Number of Problems by Income Levels*				
	$900 to $1,600	*$1,600 to $2,300*	*$2,300 to $3,000*	*$900 to $3,000*	*Number of Families in Each Occupational Group*
1. Food					
Professional	13.8	17.8	19.6	17.5	20
Commercial	9.2	14.2	16.9	13.9	25
Industrial	9.6	14.2	18.5	13.9	30
Total average	10.3	15.2	18.2	14.2	75
2. Clothing					
Professional	4.2	7.7	8.8	7.3	20
Commercial	3.5	6.8	7.0	6.0	25
Industrial	1.4	5.2	6.4	3.8	30
Total average	2.6	6.4	7.4	5.4	75
3. Housing and Equipment					
Professional	5.6	5.8	6.7	6.1	20
Commercial	5.8	5.2	5.9	5.5	25
Industrial	3.6	5.9	6.4	5.0	30
Total average	4.5	5.6	6.3	5.5	75
4. Health and Recreation					
Professional	2.0	2.0	2.0	2.0	20
Commercial	1.8	1.2	1.5	1.5	25
Industrial	1.7	1.9	1.7	1.8	30
Total average	1.8	1.7	1.7	1.7	75
5. Children and Education					
Professional	2.8	2.4	2.5	2.6	20
Commercial	2.4	3.2	3.7	3.2	25
Industrial	2.7	3.2	3.7	3.1	30
Total average	2.6	3.0	3.3	3.0	75
6. Insurance and Investment					
Professional	4.0	4.5	4.3	4.5	20
Commercial	4.2	3.8	3.4	3.7	25
Industrial	2.9	3.5	3.5	3.2	30
Total average	3.4	3.9	3.9	3.7	75

TABLE 45 (*Continued*)

Topic and Group	*Average Number of Problems by Income Levels*				
	$900 to $1,600	*$1,600 to $2,300*	*$2,300 to $3,000*	*$900 to $3,000*	*Number of Families in Each Occupational Group*
7. Wages and Employment					
Professional	1.6	2.0	2.6	3.1	20
Commercial	2.1	1.6	2.1	1.9	25
Industrial	2.1	2.8	2.5	2.4	30
Total average	2.0	2.2	2.4	2.2	75
8. General Economic Problems					
Professional	8.6	10.0	11.0	10.0	20
Commercial	9.2	8.8	8.6	8.8	25
Industrial	6.6	9.0	13.3	9.0	30
Total average	7.7	9.2	10.7	9.2	75
9. General Problems in Household Buying					
Professional	6.0	7.2	7.6	7.1	20
Commercial	4.8	7.0	6.9	6.3	25
Industrial	4.3	6.0	6.1	5.3	30
Total average	4.8	6.6	6.9	6.1	75
All Topics					
Professional	48.6	57.6	66.0	59.5	20
Commercial	43.0	52.2	56.0	51.1	25
Industrial	35.2	51.7	62.5	47.1	30
Total average	40.0	54.1	60.0	51.3	75

of families have averaged more problems than either the commercial or the industrial group at the income range $900–$3,000. The array also shows that all groups average more problems per family as the income increases.

Within each of the nine topic divisions the professional group of families average more problems per family on each of the three income levels than either of the other two groups, with the exception of topic 4, health and recreation, and topic 5, children and education, where all average practically the same number of problems irrespective of income or occupation. In topic 7, wages and employment, the professional group does not average as many

TABLE 46

NUMBER OF PROBLEMS ON THE 9 TOPICS RAISED BY FAMILIES OF DIFFERENT SIZES AT INCOME RANGE $900–$3,000

Topics and Number of Children in Family	*Average Number of Problems Raised*		*Number of Families Represented*	
	$900–$3,000			
1. Foods and Food Buying				
2 children	14.8		43	
3 children	14.6		25	
4 children	15.3		7	
		14.6		75
2. Clothing				
2 children	5.7		42	
3 children	5.2		24	
4 children	4.5		7	
		5.4		73
3. Housing and Equipment				
2 children	5.2		43	
3 children	4.5		25	
4 children	7.5		7	
		5.5		75
4. Health and Recreation				
2 children	1.6		42	
3 children	1.8		25	
4 children	2.4		7	
		1.7		74
5. Children and Education				
2 children	2.5		42	
3 children	3.2		24	
4 children	5.1		7	
		3.1		73
6. Insurance and Investments				
2 children	4.0		43	
3 children	3.2		25	
4 children	3.5		7	
		3.7		75
7. Wages and Employment				
2 children	2.3		41	
3 children	2.0		24	
4 children	1.2		5	
		2.2		70

TABLE 46 (*Continued*)

Topics and Number of Children in Family	*Average Number of Problems Raised*	
	$900–$3,000	*Number of Families Represented*
8. General Economic Problems		
2 children	9.2	43
3 children	9.0	25
4 children	8.5	7
	9.2	75
9. General Problems in Household Buying		
2 children	6.0	43
3 children	6.0	25
4 children	6.5	7
	6.1	75
All Topics		
2 children	51.9	43
3 children	50.9	25
4 children	55.0	7 75

problems on the $900–$1,600 and $1,600–$2,300 income levels as the industrial group of families.

Table 46 shows that the 43 families with 2 children average 51.9 problems, while the 25 families with 3 children and the 7 families with 4 children average 50.9 and 55.0 problems, respectively. This indicates that families with more children have more problems. In the topics dealing with housing and with children and education the number of problems raised by families with 4 children exceeds markedly the number of problems raised by families with 2 or 3 children. There is no marked difference in the number of problems raised by families of different sizes in the other 7 topic divisions.

Table 47 shows that there are 31 women who had from 6 months to 2 years of home economics training while they were in school. This means that some of these women had such home economics as was given in the public school system from five to fifteen years ago. All of these women have been married from four to fifteen or sixteen years. During this time there has been a change in the type of home economics work given in the schools. The older group of women had the type of training which was made up

TABLE 47

NUMBER OF PROBLEMS RAISED BY FAMILIES WHERE THE WIFE HAS HAD SOME HOME ECONOMICS TRAINING COMPARED WITH NUMBER OF PROBLEMS RAISED BY FAMILIES WHERE THE WIFE DID NOT HAVE SUCH TRAINING

	Number of Women with Home Economic Training	*Average Number of Problems Raised on All Topics*
$900–$1,600		
Wife had had from 6 months to 2 years of home economics	14	42.2
Wife had had no home economics training	11	37.2
$1,600–$2,300		
With home economics	9	49.4
Without home economics	16	56.8
$2,300–$3,000		
With home economics	8	62.7
Without home economics	17	64.0
Total		
With home economics	31	51.4
Without home economics	44	52.6

entirely of cooking and sewing, while the younger groups have had some training in the newer home economics work which includes child care and family relationships. In checking the numbers of the actual problems raised by the groups, one finds that there is an equal distribution of all 126 problems between each of the two groups, indicating that certain problems are not raised to the exclusion of others by one group.

SUMMARY

Among the 75 families interviewed the amount of income was a poor index of taste. Throughout all the interviews one could not fail to notice that the differences in expenditure between income groups were differences in degree to a greater extent than they were differences in kind. The most striking thing about the comparisons between income levels and occupational groups is not the differences but the similarities in interests.

As the income increases the 126 problems occur more frequently among the families on each of the three income levels. However, when the problems are separated by topics those dealing with health and recreation, children and education, insurance and investment, and wages and employment occur the same number of times on each income level.

The professional group of families averages more problems than either the commercial or the industrial group. However, the problems on topic 4, health and recreation, and topic 5, children and education, occur the same number of times among families regardless of income or occupation.

Families with 4 children average more problems than families with 2 or 3 children, but this difference is due to the many more problems occurring among the larger families in topics dealing with housing and with children and education. Among the other 7 topics the size of the family does not seem to make any decided difference in the number of problems raised by these families.

There is an equal distribution of problems among the families where the wife had some home economics training before marriage and those where the wife had not received this training. There is no difference in the number or type of the problems raised by the older or the younger group of women who had had home economics training.

PART III

CHAPTER XIV

PROBLEMS EMERGING FROM THE INTERVIEWS ARRANGED IN RANK ORDER OF FREQUENCY FOR COMPARISON WITH JURY EVALUATION

A jury of 75 graduate students and professors of home economics evaluated the 126 problems on the basis of the importance of these problems in relation to the particular group of families interviewed when their income possibilities were considered. The following rating scale was used:

1—highly important.
2—of second-rate importance relatively.
3—of relatively little importance.
0—of practically no importance for the group concerned.

Problems checked 1 by the jury were multiplied by 3, problems marked 2 were multiplied by 2, and those marked 3 were multiplied by 1 and then totaled. The highest possible total would be 4.

The 126 problems as rated by the jury were placed in rank order for comparison with the rank order of importance indicated by the members of families raising the problems within each of the three income levels. Thus, for example, one finds that problem 1, which was raised by 61 out of the total 75 families, was raised more times than any other problem by families on the lowest income level but was not considered of as much importance by families on the middle income level. There are 9 problems—numbers 1, 2, 3, 5, 6, 13, 17, 23, 26—that were raised an equal number of times by families on the $1,600–$2,300 income level, which gives them a ranking of 7. In the highest income level, $2,300–$3,000, problem 1 falls to the twentieth place. The jury placed problems 1 and 67 among the most important problems.

It is interesting to note that all problems raised most frequently by the families on the lowest income level relate to immediate problems which might be solved if the families had more definite information regarding food values, clothing, or health and housing conditions. The families on the highest income level raise these same problems but not as frequently. They raise more general problems before they bring up the specific ones. The middle income level, $1,600–$2,300, maintains a balance between the lowest and the highest income level.

Summary

1. Families on the lowest income level, $900–$1,600, raise specific problems which might be solved by more definite information regarding food values, child care, and housing conditions more frequently than other problems.

2. Families on the highest income level, $2,300–$3,000, show interest in general problems before they do in the more specific ones.

3. Families on the middle income level, $1,600–$2,300, do not show marked interest in either the specific or the general problems. Their interests were more evenly divided between practical and theoretical problems than either of the other two groups.

4. The jury judged the importance of these problems not only from the standpoint of their importance to the families when one considers their income possibilities, but also from the point of view of the classroom teacher. They placed many of the more theoretical problems ahead of the more immediate or practical problems. This may be due to the confusion of looking at the problem from the point of view of the person raising it and from the point of view of the person looking at it from the outside.

Table 48 shows the 126 problems arranged for comparison with the jury judgment.

TABLE 48

PROBLEMS EMERGING FROM THE INTERVIEWS ARRANGED IN RANK ORDER OF FREQUENCY WITHIN INCOME LEVELS FOR COMPARISON WITH JURY EVALUATION

Men and Women with Incomes from $900 to $3,000 Wanted to Know:	*Problems in Rank Order of Frequency by 25 Families on Each Income Level and by Jury Evaluation*			
	$900 to $1,600	*$1,600 to $2,300*	*$2,300 to $3,000*	*Jury Judgment*
1. More about the nutritive value of food and its relation to the cost.	1	7	20	1.5
2. Where parents could obtain aid in placing their children in better paying positions than their own.	8.5	7	7	25.5
3. What is causing the present business depression.	8.5	7	11.5	82
4. Why knowledge of birth control, for both social and economic reasons, should not be more easily obtainable. (Hygienic aspects as well as economic.)	4.5	1	34	20
5. Why food prices fluctuate so much more than prices of other household commodities.	8.5	7	14	76
6. What constructive work is being done to equalize wages and cost of living; if employers should not feel greater responsibility for increasing wages when living costs increase.	14	7	20	36.5
7. More about tenant rights under a lease.	14	25	20	4
8. If there is any way for a tenant to get redress without great expense if the terms of the lease are not followed.	14	25	20	165
9. What is the basis for determining rents.	14	25	20	13
10. Why the rich should not be taxed more heavily to secure more nearly equal distribution of incomes and opportunity.	4.5	13.5	45.5	92.5
11. What quantities of food to buy in order to save money.	4.5	18.5	45.5	16.5
12. What institutions or agencies are making a direct contribution to the household.	19	18.5	24.5	34
13. More about the quality of hosiery from the label.	38	7	7	32
14. Why poverty must exist; why there is not a more nearly equal distribution of money.	19	36	20	85
15. What is the basis for determining premiums for insurance.	25.5	13.5	24.5	74
16. How much insurance one should carry on a given income.	19	31.5	24.5	27

TABLE 48 (*Continued*)

Men and Women with Incomes from $900 to $3,000 Wanted to Know:	*Problems in Rank Order of Frequency by 25 Families on Each Income Level and by Jury Evaluation*			
	$900 to $1,600	*$1,600 to $2,300*	*$2,300 to $3,000*	*Jury Judgment*
17. If parents are not justified in requiring their children who still live with them after beginning to earn money to pay for room and board.	38	7	11.5	61
18. What to substitute for meat in order to save money and obtain the same nutritive value.	2	31.5	52.5	6
19. Why the United States is called such a prosperous country when there is so much poverty and unemployment.	19	36	20	82
20. More about European forms of social insurance.	8.5	31.5	45.5	99
21. Where to obtain non-technical information on food values of use in buying, and in planning menus.	38	18.5	7	40
22. More about the relative wearing qualities of materials used for underwear.	61	13.5	2.5	12
23. How much reliance to place in nationally advertised hosiery.	72	7	7	22
24. The proper proportion of money to spend for food.	78.5	17	1	32
25. How to judge the proportion of edible to non-edible food and its relation to the cost.	7.5	25	78	35
26. Where one could get information about the various terms used for hosiery (service, sheer, etc.).	86	7	7	92.5
27. How to take advantage of sales, and if there is a saving of money in the initial cost at the expense of quality.	8.5	25	78	16.5
28. What are the federal and state regulations for foods.	72	18.5	7	110.5
29. More about the economics of installment buying.	.9	49	39	24
30. More about the difference between food bought in bulk and food bought in packages.	72	25	7	46.5
31. What local control the Department of Health exerts over food stores. Relationship between prices of the goods and the higher standards of the stores.	29.5	31.5	39	69
32. How much of one's income one is justified in paying for rent.	72	13.5	20	9

TABLE 48 (*Continued*)

Men and Women with Incomes from $900 to $3,000 Wanted to Know:	*Problems in Rank Order of Frequency by 25 Families on Each Income Level and by Jury Evaluation*			
	$900 to $1,600	*$1,600 to $2,300*	*$2,300 to $3,000*	*Jury Judgment*
33. What type or types of insurance are the best investment for one with a limited income.	38	31.5	24.5	4
34. Whether one can tell definitely how much machinery is causing unemployment by displacing men.	23.5	41	52.5	108
35. How present inheritance laws could be changed to produce a more nearly equal distribution of money.	14	41	78	122
36. The significance of the different types of markets.	38	2	86.5	90
37. How the consumer can be sure that the dealer is selling a good grade of food commodities, such as meat.	72	18.5	34	36.5
38. If one is justified in borrowing on one's insurance policy for other than necessities.	29.5	41	52.5	28.5
39. Why certain stores can offer cut rates, and the effect on other stores.	38	36	45.5	82
40. What is the method of financing a coöperative apartment.	38	41	45.5	115.5
41. How parents could prevent children from leaving school as soon as possible to work; and if their remaining in school longer would not make for greater prosperity.	44.5	41	39	36.5
42. Varieties of food on the market.	61	49	24.5	73
43. Why labels do not tell the consumer what she needs to know (use, quality, amount, etc.).	38	41	52.5	70
44. When foods are in season, such as fresh fruits and vegetables	50	45	39	46.5
45. Why public employment bureaus are so inadequate.	25.5	69	58.5	87.5
46. How to judge durability of textile materials.	22	61	78	4
47. Comparative prices and food values of fresh, dried, and canned fruits.	50	41	58.5	25.5
48. The possibilities of reducing food costs through coöperative buying.	78.5	61	14	78
49. Where to obtain information about weights and measures.	61	49	39	104
50. Proper proportion of the income to spend for clothes.	122.5	25	24.5	16.5

TABLE 48 (*Continued*)

Men and Women with Incomes from $900 to $3,000 Wanted to Know:	*Problems in Rank Order of Frequency by 25 Families on Each Income Level and by Jury Evaluation*			
	$900 to $1,600	*$1,600 to $2,300*	*$2,300 to $3,000*	*Jury Judgment*
51. How much extensive advertising of a food product affects its price.	116	61	25	101
52. How much a brand name insures a standardized quality of goods.	105	31.5	45.5	59.5
53. If recipes and household suggestions in newspapers and magazines are reliable; if they are not for people of means.	72	61	34	90
54. What are the chief sources of the important foods, and how the source influences quality and price.	61	102.5	14	103
55. Which cuts of meat are most economical, considering price, nutritive value, and amount of fuel needed to cook them.	29.5	61	68	12
56. The relation between nutritive values and prices of raw, evaporated, and condensed milk.	29.5	61	68	22
57. What justification there is for the lower wages of women.	29.5	72.5	68	67
58. More about the relation between school laws and child labor laws.	23.5	61	96	43
59. How a tariff affects food prices.	50	93.5	39	124
60. More about the original cost of food bought in the market and its cost when ready for consumption.	72	49	58.5	120.5
61. How much actual saving there is in the home preparation of food; for example, bread.	50	49	61	66
62. How much the practice of exchange and return of textile goods affects prices.	94	61	24.5	59.5
63. What are the relative food values of meat and fish, and what is the reason for the difference in cost.	50	49	78	39
64. Why the labels on canned fruits and vegetables do not tell more about the contents.	105	61	24.5	96.5
65. Whether it would not lower food prices to buy direct from the producer.	122.5	49	24.5	94.5
66. More about the keeping qualities of food and their relation to the amount to buy.	61	61	62.5	39
67. How to determine what are efficient household utensils.	38	72.5	78	1.5

TABLE 48 (*Continued*)

Men and Women with Incomes from $900 to $3,000 Wanted to Know:	*Problems in Rank Order of Frequency by 25 Families on Each Income Level and by Jury Evaluation*			
	$900 to $1,600	*$1,600 to $2,300*	*$2,300 to $3,000*	*Jury Judgment*
68. Why the worker should not be allowed to spend money for alcoholic drinks when he does not drink immoderately.	38	72.5	78	1.5
69. What is a woman's time in the home worth.	61	76.5	62.5	32
70. What general connection exists between the terms—tariff, monopoly, public utilities—and the individual household.	61	81.5	62.5	112
71. More about the various sizes of canned goods.	61	61	78	64
72. More about the relationship of price and quality.	50	61	86.5	114
73. If it is possible for the consumer to get better style and quality at lower prices.	61	182.5	52.5	43
74. More about the public health resources available to those who cannot afford full medical costs.	38	72.5	96	7
75. More about the economics of having clothes cleaned professionally.	105	61	52.5	55
76. More about the different brands of canned goods on the market.	86	81.5	52.5	52.5
77. Whether home sewing is an economy in the long run if what one might earn otherwise is considered.	50	81.5	78	71
78. Whether trading at one satisfactory store would tend to eliminate competition and affect food prices.	105	81.5	39	12
79. More about the proportion of money to spend for outside clothes, underwear, shoes, etc.	86	61	68	87.5
80. More about the present regulation for grading food products.	86	81.5	58.5	39
81. How to identify the chief fabrics sold by the yard.	86	61	78	85
82. The effects of cold storage on the price of food.	38	93.5	103.5	45
83. If the equipping of a kitchen from a five-and-ten-cent store does not cost more in the end.	61	102.5	78	79
84. What is the distinction between old age insurance and old age pension.	78.5	72.5	90	30

TABLE 48 (*Continued*)

Men and Women with Incomes from $900 to $3,000 Wanted to Know:	*Problems in Rank Order of Frequency by 25 Families on Each Income Level and by Jury Evaluation*			
	$900 to $1,600	*$1,600 to $2,300*	*$2,300 to $3,000*	*Jury Judgment*
85. What is the effect on food prices of paying cash or obtaining credit.	86	81.5	78	12
86. How to make comparable figures of the cost of living in Manhattan and in a suburb.	122.5	81.5	52.5	52.5
87. What effect has the extensive sale of accessories on the employment situation, prices, etc.	122.5	61	68	119
88. The effect of cold storage on the nutritive value of food.	50	93.5	103.5	43
89. What causes fluctuations in prices in general.	86	81.5	86.5	22
90. Arguments for and against husbands and wives sharing equally in household expenses. (On the wife's working full or part time.)	86	102.5	68	72
91. How can one plan to buy systematically if income is uncertain; if there should not be unemployment insurance to prevent haphazard buying.	78.5	72.5	96	54
92. What is meant by public revenues; how they are obtained, and the relation they bear to free parks, etc.	44.5	106.5	96	105
93. More about the organization of the Stock Exchange.	116	81.5	62.5	126
94. How schools can afford to give children so much in the way of free clinics.	61	81.5	110.5	62
95. If overspecialization is not one of the great difficulties in the way of a skilled laborer's finding employment in the present business depression.	105	93.5	78	99
96. Arguments why women should carry insurance.	50	93.5	113.5	58
97. What are the distinctions between speculation, gambling, and investments.	86	81.5	96	76
98. More about housing conditions and health.	94	93.5	90	8
99. More about the influence various sizes of cooking utensils have on the amount of fuel consumed.	86	93.5	103.5	50.5
100. What is meant by household capital goods.	61	109.5	103.5	102
101. Whether an adequate old age pension system would not be a good investment of public funds.	72	109.5	96	80

TABLE 48 (*Continued*)

Men and Women with Incomes from $900 to $3,000 Wanted to Know:	*Problems in Rank Order of Frequency by 25 Families on Each Income Level and by Jury Evaluation*			
	$900 to $1,600	*$1,600 to $2,300*	*$2,300 to $3,000*	*Jury Judgment*
102. How the publication of foods prices in newspapers affects the consumer.	94	93.5	103.5	90
103. Whether the efficient functioning of the Farm Board will result in a radical lowering of food costs.	105	102.5	96	117.5
104. The relation between cold storage and food distribution.	112.5	81.5	96	115.5
105. Whether groups of people who adhere closely to racial customs buy in large enough quantities to influence market distribution. (Example: the Italians who demand imported cheese and sauces.)	72	109.5	110.5	125
106. What justification stores have for charging more in certain sections of the city even though rents may be similar in the various sections.	105	93.5	110.5	99
107. More about the prices and the wearing qualities of furs.	116	93.5	103.5	94.5
108. Whether there is not some way to provide medical service at lower cost for those in moderate circumstances.	116	113.5	86.5	12
109. How mass production and standardization of articles, such as felt hats, affects the price.	122.5	102.5	96	96.5
110. What is meant by the purchasing power of the dollar. What is meant by the changing value of the dollar.	105	113.5	90	50.5
111. How to buy ready-to-serve food so as to get the most for the money.	122.5	93.5	110.5	46
112. If there would be any radical lowering of prices if women's clothes were as standardized as men's are.	105	106.5	113.5	108
113. If one should live in what seems an undesirable neighborhood in order to maintain an insurance policy.	86	113.5	113.5	56.6
114. If employment conditions could not be shown on the label so the consumer might have a chance to buy only goods made under the best conditions.	61	117	125	76
115. Why schools do not give more information that will help children to make a better living (that is, higher wages).	105	122	110.5	49

TABLE 48 (*Continued*)

Men and Women with Incomes from $900 to $3,000 Wanted to Know:	*Problems in Rank Order of Frequency by 25 Families on Each Income Level and by Jury Evaluation*			
	$900 to $1,600	*$1,600 to $2,300*	*$2,300 to $3,000*	*Jury Judgment*
116. Why parents are always being asked to contribute to various school enterprises when schools are supposed to be free.	105	122	110.5	106
117. What effect the present restriction of immigration will have on the labor market eventually.	105	109.5	118	108
118. Why schools do not teach children to use leisure time in a more constructive way. (Criticism of children's attitude toward school and holidays.)	94	117	118	28.5
119. More about the economic relation between a shorter working week and increased leisure; and if the increased leisure would not cost the working man more, because of greater opportunity to acquire more expensive habits.	116	117	115.5	65
120. In what ways the city zoning laws directly affect the individual families.	105	113.5	121.5	85
121. How much money one is justified in spending for amusement when the necessary food and clothing take practically all of one's money.	94	122	121.5	19
122. How far competition regulates prices and wages; how far monopolistic control regulates them.	105	122	121.5	123
123. How can the capitalist class justify the statement that the United States offers equal opportunities.	105	122	121.5	113
124. If there is any possibility that milk, will, like gas, be declared a public utility.	122.5	122	118	117.5
125. Whether consumers' clubs as advocated by Chase and Schlink will ever be developed in a practical way.	105	122	125	110.5
126. What is meant by the saying that the prosperity of the country depends upon the inequality of incomes, since this makes for greater capital accumulation.	105	126	125	120.5

CHAPTER XV

INTERPRETATION AND APPLICATIONS

As stated in Chapter I, this study was undertaken to find out, through personal interviews with selected families, problems the solution of which would aid in securing a more efficient use of their incomes, better household management, and thereby a higher standard of living. It was assumed that a large part of the waste of our economic order arises, even after goods have been produced, from poorly arranged consumption which results in the loss of satisfactions and enjoyment on the part of those who consume poorly. Consumption was defined as the science which deals with the administration of resources for the satisfaction of human wants, in so far as this administration involves consideration of prices or cost. A standard of living was defined as the sum total, not only of material things, but of satisfactions.

The 126 problems which emerge from the interviews with the 75 families show that some of the errors of consumption are due to the nature of the economic order in which the consumer finds himself, and some to the imitation of the consumption of others without proper allowance for the different circumstances under which consumption takes place. Other mistakes are due to lack of knowledge on the part of consumers and in many cases to lack of pride in efficient consumption. The problems emerging from the interviews show that the consumer needs education in the right ways of living. Education of the consumer, as such, is greatly neglected. He is trained in cultural subjects and occasionally in vocational lines which will provide him with a means of making an income; but there is little in our present curricula which teaches him how to use that income wisely once it has been acquired. The conflict between producers and consumers is at present entirely to the advantage of producers. The modern producer studies the consumer, not as a human being but as a prospective purchaser. Few of to-day's producers would risk years of waiting to educate consumers to some good thing that might begin to pay one hundred years hence. That is one reason why governments must take a hand in providing such things as museums and parks for the people.

The consumer is expected to pick up from his family life and environment the knowledge necessary to live wisely. He suffers a disadvantage because in many cases he does not know what he needs, and in consequence is susceptible to the advertisers who spend millions of dollars annually trying to persuade him to buy what they want to sell rather than what he needs. As long as the consumer is unable to judge the performance of commodities before their purchase he will be sold commodities unsuited to his needs and of lower qualities than he believes he is buying. One remedy which has been suggested for this situation is the standardization of commodities and of commodity performance. Many of the 75 families represented in this study mention the possible benefits of standardization.

The problems raised by these families show how little they know about the most economical kinds of food to buy or the best ways of preparing them, or about the kind of housing and furnishings which make for attractive and healthful homes. The problem of clothing, which is common to all people, is left to the dictates of fashion regardless of taste and the need of comfort and protection.

The newer type of home economics training is working along the lines that "homemaking is the joint contribution of all members of the family group, working toward the maximum of natural development, capacity for mental enrichment, and social efficiency of all, according to their needs."[1]

The problems listed in this study should be of value in determining the content for a course which will help both men and women to a realization of their responsibilities as consumers and homemakers. Many of these problems show how little the families interviewed know of their relationship to the community; but the fact that these problems were raised shows that these people do feel that there is a relationship, and that the family is a part of a larger group, the community. These 126 problems should be of value as suggestive of problems which might interest other communities.

The technique used in this study may be employed in any community. By its use local problems and needs may be found as questions to be answered by the content of the curriculum made to meet

[1] Hader, Mathilde C., "A Possible Scheme for Coördination in Education for Homemaking," *Teachers College Record*, April, 1930, p. 663.

the needs of the people of that locality. At the same time one could discover the opportunities for adult education after school, since the problems in this study show the point of view of adults engaged in homemaking rather than the point of view of students and teachers. The material should be useful in connection with the budget studies which are being made from time to time for various income groups and income levels. These problems should be used as complementary material to such a study as Harap's *Education of the Consumer*,[2] which lists educational objectives from the standpoint of what statistics show are the present consumption habits of the people. His study reflects American economic life in that it shows what the people collectively do consume. The present study shows what a section of the people would like to know more about in order to improve their standards of living.

From the investigation arise the questions which a curriculum in the economics of the home for prospective homemakers of the type studied in New York City should provide content to answer. Also, that in any community those questions raised by this study which are common to all homemakers, together with others which might be found by the use of this method of inquiry for any particular community, are the questions for which answers should be provided in a curriculum on economics of the home for that community.

Both in revealing questions on problems which represent common needs for all homemakers and in developing and demonstrating a method for finding the needs peculiar to any community, this investigation contributes to a determination of a basis for building a course on the economics of the home. This is the purpose for which the investigation was undertaken.

[2] Harap, Henry, *Education of the Consumer*. Macmillan, New York, 1924.

APPENDIX

SCHEDULE USED AS GUIDE FOR THE INTERVIEWS

Schedule No. ....
Visitor ....
Date of Visit ....

FAMILY CENSUS	Sex	Age	Birthplace	Date of Marriage	Occupation
Man	..X..	....	....	....	....
Wife	..X..	....	....	....	....
Child	......	....	....	....	....
Child	......	....	....	....	....
Roomer	......	....	.....X.....	....X....	....
Others	......	....	.....X.....	....X....	....
....	......	....	.....X.....	....X....	....

HOUSING FACTS: Tenement..........Apartment..........Coöperative Apartment..........Elevator..........Rent paid by the month $..........How long living in present place..........Rent in last place $..........Does present rent include furnishings..........light..........heat..........hot water..........telephone..........kitchen stove..........gas..........electric..........coal..........refrigerator..........

EDUCATION	Man	Wife	Child	Child	Comments
Graduated from or in at present					
Name of School	......	......	......	......	....
Expenses					
tuition	......	......	......	......	....
books	......	......	......	......	....
supplies	......	......	......	......	....
carfare	......	......	......	......	....
other	......	......	......	......	....
Special lessons					
music	......	......	......	......	....
....	......	......	......	......	....
....	......	......	......	......	....
Daily papers					
....	......	......	......	......	....
Magazine list					
....	......	......	......	......	....
Books					
....	......	......	......	......	....
Lectures					
....	......	......	......	......	....

Amusements, Leisure, Recreation	Man	Wife	Child	Child	Cost	Average No. Times wk.mo.yr.	Comments
Moving pictures							
Theatre							
Dances							
Pool—Billiards							
Parties at home							
cost of refreshments							
other							
Sports							
baseball							
Concerts							
Radio							
upkeep							
Phonograph							
cost of records							
Vacations							
Pleasure trips							
Musical instruments played at home							

Automobile: Upkeep..........insurance..........tax..........license......
accidents..........garage..........gas, etc. ....
How many use the car?..........
Is it used only for business?..........proportion of time ¼........
½..........¾..........
Is it used only for pleasure?..........proportion of time ¼........
½..........¾..........
Approximate mileage for the year..........Does this include vacation trip?..........
Make of the car..........Year......

House Operation	Amount wk.mo.yr.	Cost wk.mo.yr.	Total Cost Comments
Light	....	....	....
Fuel and heat	....	....	....
Ice	....	....	....
Telephone	....	....	....
Service—			
cleaning	....	....	....
laundry	....	....	....
cooking	....	....	....
sewing	....	....	....
other	....	....	....
Garage removal	....	....	....
House cleaning	....	....	....
supplies, soap, etc.	....	....	....
....	....	....	....
....	....	....	....
Laundry supplies	....	....	....
Others	....	....	....
....	....	....	....

Do you do all your own work?..........How long does it take you each day for cooking?..........for care of rooms?.........Do your children help? ....Your husband?..........

Did you have home economics in school?..........Cooking?..........Sewing? ....Home management?..........Which courses helped you the most?..........Other courses that helped.............................. ....

Do newspapers give you any help in your housekeeping?......What help?......

Do magazines?..........List magazines...................................

Do you feel that you need help in buying food?..........Clothing?.......... Furnishings?..........

In what way do you need help (that is) When to buy?..........Where to buy? ....Quantity?..........Quality?..........

Furnishings and Equipment	Cost	Where Bought Type of Store	Reasons for Buying Addition or Replacement
Furniture			
1. Refrigerator	....	....	....
2. Tables	....	....	....
3. Chairs	....	....	....
4. Rugs	....	....	....
5. Sewing Machine	....	....	....
6. Davenport	....	....	....
7. Buffet	....	....	....
8. Piano—Radio	....	....	....
9. Bed	....	....	....
Electrical Equipment			
10. Iron	....	....	....
11.	....	....	....
12.	....	....	....
Bedding			
13. Mattresses	....	....	....
14. Blankets	....	....	....
15. Comforts	....	....	....
16. Spreads	....	....	....
17. Pillows	....	....	....
18. Sheets	....	....	....
19. Pillow cases	....	....	....
20.	....	....	....
Linen			
21. Towels	....	....	....
22. Napkins	....	....	....
23. Table cloths	....	....	....
24. Curtains	....	....	....
25.	....	....	....

Which of the articles did you buy

(A) because you knew they would last well?............................

(B) because the price was right for you?..............................

(C) because someone had recommended it?............................

(D) because your neighbor had one?..................................

(E) would you replace with the same?..................................

(F) other reasons?...

FOOD

Number of meals provided at home.........per week......per month.........
Number of meals bought out...............per week......per month.........
Number of visitors for meals...............per week......per month.........
Do the children eat lunches at school?.......How many?...Average cost.......
Does your husband carry his lunch?......Number of times per week?......pay lunch, cost......

	Amount wk.mo.yr.	Cost	Type of Store Where Purchased	Buying Habits—Amounts Purchased, etc.
Bread	....	....	....	....
Cake	....	....	....	....
Crackers	....	....	....	....
Butter	....	....	....	....
Eggs	....	....	....	....
Milk	....	....	....	....
Cream	....	....	....	....
Dry Groceries	....	....	....	....
....	....	....	....	....
....	....	....	....	....
....	....	....	....	....
Fruit	....	....	....	....
....	....	....	....	....
....	....	....	....	....
Vegetables	....	....	....	....
....	....	....	....	....
....	....	....	....	....
Meat	....	....	....	....
....	....	....	....	....
....	....	....	....	....
Canned Goods	....	....	....	....
....	....	....	....	....
....	....	....	....	....
....	....	....	....	....

Amount of milk per day..........vegetables..........fruits..........
Do you watch market prices in newspapers?.............................
Do you compare prices for some goods in different types of stores?..............
Do you belong to a coöperative buying club?........Amount of saving?........

CLOTHING	Man	Wife	Child	Child	Comments as to Buying Habits
Outer Clothing					
....	......	......	......	......	....
....	......	......	......	......	....
....	......	......	......	......	....
....	......	......	......	......	....
....	......	......	......	......	....
....	......	......	......	......	....
....	......	......	......	......	....
....	......	......	......	......	....
....	......	......	......	......	....
Underwear					
....	......	......	......	......	....
....	......	......	......	......	....
....	......	......	......	......	....
....	......	......	......	......	....
....	......	......	......	......	....
Accessories					
....	......	......	......	......	....
....	......	......	......	......	....
....	......	......	......	......	....
....	......	......	......	......	....
....	......	......	......	......	....
Upkeep of Clothing					
cleaning	......	......	......	......	....
pressing	......	......	......	......	....
other	......	......	......	......	....
laundry	......	......	......	......	....

Sewing at Home: Do you buy clothes expecting them to last more than one season?............

Do you buy during sales?..................................

Do you compare the relative cost of home-made and ready-made garments?..........

Do you have a definite written plan for buying?..........
Mental plan?..........

Personal Expenses	Man	Wife	Child	Child	Comments
Carfare	......	......	......	......	....
Contributions					
church	......	......	......	......	....
philanthropic	......	......	......	......	....
community chest	......	......	......	......	....
Tobacco					
cigars, cigarettes	......	......	......	......	....
Gifts					
Christmas	......	......	......	......	....
birthday	......	......	......	......	....
wedding	......	......	......	......	....
sick friends	......	......	......	......	....
other	......	......	......	......	....
Barbers, Hairdressers	......	......	......	......	....
Candy	......	......	......	......	....
Chewing Gum	......	......	......	......	....
Cosmetics	......	......	......	......	....
Other	......	......	......	......	....
....	......	......	......	......	....
Health					
physician	......	......	......	......	....
dentist	......	......	......	......	....
eyeglasses	......	......	......	......	....
patent medicines	......	......	......	......	....
drugs	......	......	......	......	....
other	......	......	......	......	....

INVESTMENTS, SAVINGS, INSURANCE, INCOME

Real Estate..............Stocks............Bonds............Others.......
Savings Banks..................................
Insurance.........................kind as, life (kind of life insurance)..........
accident................other............
How many times your present income do you want saved before you retire?........
What provision are you making for old age?..................................
What provision are you making for children's education?......................
Are you saving some money regularly?..................
Income
Present income...................is
from man...................from wife..........from children..........
from roomers.................from lodgers......from other sources......
income tax...................
What was the income when married?....................
How long have you had the present income?.............
How much money had been saved before marriage?.......
Had the wife worked as a wage-earner before marriage?......length of time?......
wages?......
Has the wife worked since marriage?........How long?........Why?........
Wages..........Full time..........Part time..........
Does the husband give his wife an allowance?.....give the whole amount? ....
other divisions......
Who makes decisions in regard to the division of money? Husband?......Wife?..
....Together?......
Are the children given an allowance?......How much?......
How long have children had an allowance?..........
What source of income would you have during disability?.....................
Does the man have a secondary occupation as a resort for the support of the family
in case of accident with primary one?......What is it?......................